Praise for

THE BRIEF

"I personally witnessed Rich's passion for helping our interns and new graduates transition from school to working in a large corporation. He spent a lot of time mentoring and advising them and I know it has made a difference in their careers. As I said when Rich decided to retire and pursue his passion, he left a legacy behind that he could be proud of. Many of the folks he coached are now in leadership positions and they can thank Rich for putting them on the right path. *The Brief* gives Rich the ability to continue to pass on his real-world experience and advice to college students and early career professionals."

—*Pat McMahon, VP, Corporate Supply Chain,*
Northrop Grumman

"Such a great read! After thirty-seven years in corporate America and mentoring many early career employees and aspiring executives, this book captures the true objectives, challenges and expectations of leadership. Many young folks entering corporate America from college are yearning for a focused purpose. *The Brief* and the **6 P's** provide a genuine, thoughtful view of experience that I believe will facilitate and enhance that awareness process."

—*Catherine C. Rice, Vice President Business Management,*
Aerion Supersonic

"Everyone who is serious about living the concept of continuous learning should read and keep as a trusted reference *The Brief*. It is rare that someone with the accomplishments of Rich Leo will share his first-hand experiences in such a straightforward, practical way that makes implementing the concepts of the **6 P's** so realistic. I have seen first-hand as a classmate of Rich at the Wharton school of the University of Pennsylvania how he has used these concepts throughout his career and can highly recommend this book for anyone wanting to get the most out their own professional life."

—*Robert Boyd, Founder, Boston Street Advisors*

"Rich Leo knows what he's talking about. I worked with Rich for five years, and in our company, Rich was known as 'The Oracle,' the place you went for not ANY answer, but the RIGHT answer. What I respected about Rich was that he always went the extra mile, and explained the WHY behind his reasoning—so beneficial and rare in the corporate world. Rich won't steer you wrong—the **6 P's** are a blueprint for success. Coupled with your hard work, they will make a difference in your career and life. Enjoy the ride!"

—*Mark Skinner, VP, Directed Energy, Northrop Grumman, and retired U.S. Navy Vice Admiral*

"I am so excited that Rich has taken his many years of experience and has formulated a path through his **6 P's** for college students and early career professionals to follow. His guidance and perspective will give you the insight to what it takes to successfully transition from college to corporate America. Rich was an instrumental mentor in my career and if you are not lucky enough to have someone like him at your job, then reading The Brief will be extremely beneficial in helping you navigate your way into and through the corporate system. This valuable information will serve you well, as it's very rare to get this type of knowledge and guidance. I encourage you to read *The Brief*."

—*Emily Warren, Government OEM Sales Manager, Jamaica Bearings Group*

"I have worked closely with Rich for most of my career. He is a passionate leader with a unique and powerful management style designed to develop and encourage new leaders. His commitment did not stop at the office. Over the last fifteen years or more, he was also laser focused on giving back to the next generation. Rich volunteered his time speaking at colleges and universities offering students insight and methods to prepare for life after graduation. In *The Brief*, Rich continues his investment by offering his experience, strategies and tips to guide you on your journey. You will gain a competitive advantage on your path to success while recognizing leadership when you see it."

—*Kevin Steward, Director of Business Management,*
Northrop Grumman

"Having a successful and fulfilling career is a lifelong journey and everyone needs a roadmap. Rich Leo's formula for embracing the **6 P's—Purpose, Planning, Preparation, Priorities, Persistence, and Patience** is the secret sauce to navigating both the ups and the downs of that journey. His advice is candid and yet refreshingly realistic. A must-read for students, parents, teachers and advisors! Thank you, Rich, for turning your personal passion into an advantage for our future global leaders!"

—*Dianne Baumert-Moyik, Senior Manager, External Affairs,*
Northrop Grumman

"The transition of young folks from academia to corporate America is an area underserved. Rich's passion for this topic and the desire to share his journey are evident right from the start. Colleges and universities should consider *The Brief* as part of their curriculum and corporations to assist them with their new hire acclimation and onboarding process."

—*Ted Damaskinos, General Manager, L3Harris Technologies*

THE
BRIEF

FOLLOWING THE 6P's FOR EARLY CAREER SUCCESS

RICHARD LEO

**What they didn't tell you—the inside scoop from
a former corporate America VP and CFO**

Printed in the United States of America

First Printing, 2019

ISBN 13: 978-1-7341699-1-1

Book Design by Glen M. Edelstein

CONTENTS

FOREWORD

IT WOULD BE very interesting if possible to quantitatively identify those young minds that so often possess the right skills, yet are never discovered, let alone cultivated, or are never nurtured in the proper manner or are just never given a chance. Fortunately for me, I was provided with the right mentoring, afforded excellent exposure opportunities and motivated to see what was "in the realm of the possible."

My experience at college was great. I went to a respectable business school and learned a lot about business, but little did I know, I knew very little about business! I joined Northrop Grumman Corporation (NGC) in 2008. I was lucky to join such a great company that provided some of the most advanced military defense assets in the world. My opportunity to join NGC was all due to networking. After joining Northrop Grumman, I seemed to be doing well in my position. I kept an open mind, worked hard, proved to be resourceful, but more than anything, listened and learned. Apparently, senior folks like Rich noticed it.

In 2013, I was provided the opportunity that would change my life. I started working for the executive office of a multi-billion-dollar division of which Rich was the CFO. That experience would prove to be more valuable than any MBA or other degree I could have earned. I was able to witness many executives in action and learned numerous lessons of the "do's and don'ts". I took those experiences and customized them into my own style; none of which I could have learned in my undergraduate or graduate school programs. Since that time, I have accelerated my career tenfold. I now have sole profit and loss responsibility for a multi-million-dollar program, plus I am leading capture teams' sizeable future programs.

I've been very fortunate at a young age to brief many NGC VPs, Navy Captains and Navy Admirals plus French Admirals and Generals. In addition, my PowerPoint skills or "chartsmanship" is very impressive and a direct derivative of my time spent in the executive office at NGC MAS. Rich gave me the opportunity to work with him and his team during the development of his executive briefs and often shadow him during his presentations. There is no better way to learn! It's funny because folks including leadership on my current program can tell when I make the charts. They are always simple, clear, concise, and often able to be interpreted without a voiceover if need be. (Charts have a way of growing legs sometimes and walk away without the story behind them.)

Obtaining your degree, or degrees, these days is frequently a hard requirement, but there is a significant gap that exists between academia and the reality of working in corporate America. It's too often that great students don't translate into great workers because of their lack of understanding of how the real work environment operates. *The Brief* will fill that gap.

The Brief will give you a great inside perspective into corporate America and the thought process and actions required to successfully hit the ground running. I was very fortunate to work for and be personally mentored by Rich. I highly recommend that you embrace Rich's 6 P's and the real-world advice that he gives throughout the book. He approaches the book with the same passion, enthusiasm and straightforward approach as he does when you listen to him speak.

—*Adam DeSesa, International Program Manager,*
Northrop Grumman

INTRODUCTION

Your Future—No Constraints

"If you are successful, it is because somewhere, sometime,
someone gave you a life or an idea that started you
in the right direction."

--MELINDA GATES

THE TRANSITION FROM college to corporate America is unknown territory and somewhat frustrating after attaining an education to be proud of and incurring significant costs. But what if you could follow a formula for navigating all the steps you encounter?

This formula, the **6 P's—Purpose, Planning, Preparation, Priorities, Persistence, Patience**—was instrumental to forging, shaping and accelerating my career as an executive for a major aerospace defense contractor responsible for $30+ billion in sales and 85,000 employees. I was a vice president and CFO for the company's largest division and my leadership role involved 600 business and finance professionals.

How many people can say that they worked thirty-five years for a great company that designed and manufactured the most sophisticated and coolest technology on the planet? Every day centered on innovation. It was always easy to come to work knowing that the job we were doing was so very important to the safety of the country, commercial travel and the exploration of space. In addition, the company embraced and fostered diversity of thought and always underscored the importance of a happy and healthy working culture.

Throughout my career, and most specifically, the last ten to fifteen years, I had the opportunity to work closely with CEOs, other CFOs, COOs and presidents of the company, as well as other large and small companies. I also had the honor of working with the military acquisition community at all levels, including admirals and generals.

In addition, I had been awarded the chance to attend the The Wharton School of the University of Pennsylvania, arguably one of the best business schools in the world. This afforded me the opportunity to meet, learn from, and make friends with leaders from around the world.

What does my stint in business amount to for you? Exclusive insight and the wisdom of some of the smartest leaders and innovators in our country.

The content of this book is not theory; it's real stuff involving real people. My goal is to remove the mystery and give you a sneak preview of the type of place that either you recently entered or have your heart and brain set on entering.

During the last decade of my corporate career, I was at the forefront of the company in establishing university relationships, performing extensive speaking engagements, and mentoring many early career, high-potential employees. I established numerous virtual training modules and I developed a formal mentoring program across my division that eventually took hold across the company.

I decided to retire from a great career to pursue my next passion in life: To guide and share knowledge with college students as it relates to successfully transitioning from the college world to the corporate world. I also want to have the ability to give early career business and finance professionals a clear and realistic understanding of what it takes to be successful in today's ever-changing, highly competitive corporate world.

My engagements with students from many incredible universities across the country always left me inspired, knowing that they were motivated and hungry to learn as much as they could from me during and even after my visits. I conducted my speaking engagements with the goal of making sure that I was transparent, straightforward and most of all, motivating. The sessions were always done in a relaxed setting and I strongly encouraged and created an interactive exchange versus a stuffy lecture.

The reason I'm spending my post-corporate time writing this book is due to the enormous positive feedback I've received from employees, superiors, college students, college career counselors, family and friends.

Even with all that positive encouragement, it wouldn't be happening without the persistence and continuous feedback of my son, Rich, and daughter, Jacqueline, two early career business pro millennials.

I had to learn all of these things the hard way, but when the light bulb came on, so did my career. This is my attempt to give students and early career people the keys to success.

So, what is *The Brief* besides the British action-drama highlighting the shenanigans of a mischievous lawyer, a written statement submitted in court by said lawyer, or a corporate brief? My version of *The Brief* fuses summary and scenes, or real-life situations, that you can quickly think about, learn from and hopefully, build efforts from. *The Brief* chronicles virtually everything you need to know to get on the corporate ladder, lean in, take the first step up, and dare I say, reach for the top. Even snapshots of my own life are chosen as "brief stories" to offer insight.

The Brief encompasses the most critical topics that thousands of students from large and small universities that I have spoken at (USC, UCLA, UF, UCF, Fairfield, Siena, Stonybrook, Hofstra, Adelphi, etc.) repeatedly asked me about during my presentation sessions.

The following topics are largely covered, with surprising but natural guidance in other areas:

- ◆ Career journey
- ◆ Networking
- ◆ Communication skills
- ◆ The resume; a marketing and motivational tool

- Interviewing
- Searching and selecting your first professional position
- Mentoring, coaching and advocacy
- Personal training
- Promotion and compensation process
- Leadership and teamwork
- Effectively working with your boss

This information, coupled with your personal investment, will assist you in climbing higher than your competition. The fact that you are reading *The Brief* indicates that you are the type of person who is consistently searching for knowledge that will give you a competitive advantage.

Securing your first professional position can be challenging. Once you land that job, you will quickly recognize how much there is to learn in this new environment that you will find yourself immersed in. As you enter this new world, you want to make sure that you keep your mind, eyes and ears wide open, always being inquisitive, flexible and eager to learn as much as you can... as fast as you can. Nothing worth attaining comes easy; work hard, be true to yourself, help others, take time to care for your health and wellbeing and most of all, have some fun. We live in a dynamic country with endless opportunities. Keep your perspective, stay balanced, always conduct yourself with unwavering ethics and integrity and enjoy the journey.

Finally, look to *The Brief*.

—*Richard Leo, October 2019*

CHAPTER 1

Space, Air, Land, Sea and Cyber

"Education is not the filling of a pot but the lighting of a fire."
—W.B. YEATS

I ATTENDED A small private college where I started out fairly slow academically, really not knowing what direction to go in. During those years in the late 1970s and 1980s, corporations didn't have the sophisticated technology available today and quite frankly, the corporations back then did not have the same level of expectations they presently have of their employees. Results have always been important, but they were less intense. Competition between highly educated students has also intensified tenfold in my estimation.

I did go on to graduate with a business management degree with pretty good grades. Unfortunately, I was still floundering around what I was going to do with my life.

I was fortunate to land a job with the help of my father, who knew a vice president in a local aerospace company. I didn't realize it then, but that was an outcome associated with successful networking and contacts.

Now that I had my start, I had to figure out what I needed to do to thrive in this entirely new world of corporate America. A little after two years in the company, my manager fell seriously ill and the company needed someone to go to Seattle, Washington to negotiate a sizeable business deal with others on the team. Since I worked so closely with my manager, I had the most knowledge of the product and the business deal, so by default, I became the "team leader."

The vice president of business management conveyed that the leadership team had total confidence in me. I'm sure they said that because I was their only option! I can remember the day I left for the trip like it was yesterday. My father drove me to JFK Airport in New York City during a snow storm. By the way, I was never on an airplane prior to this and I was twenty-five years old. These days, twenty-five year-olds have traveled all of Europe. *How things have changed.*

Once off the plane, getting to the hotel and communicating with anyone on my team or at home was another challenge, as there was no such thing as a smart phone or a laptop computer. Before I left for this business trip, nervous as one could possibly be, I knew I had to over-prepare for this venture I was about to encounter.

The one quality I always had was an obsession with "success." I didn't see failure as an option. *The Brief,* however, permits failure—it's not only human to make mistakes; it's human to embrace them as moments for learning and rare opportunities.

I worked with many team members for several weeks to make sure that I had everything possible to help me get through this extremely challenging assignment. I will discuss more about this in the book regarding the value I put on preparation, or I should probably say "over-preparation." I spent several weeks in Seattle at The Boeing Company, and fortunately, I soared, or "climbed high!"

I must admit that I was quite overwhelmed, but I was able to keep my composure even though I was definitely way over my head.

My director flew out to meet me and the team during the final stages to provide us clearance after I debriefed him. Other than this time, there was little interface with the exception of conference calls. *Remember, no laptops, iPads, Skype, Slack, cell phones, email, Live Meeting...oh my!* My director also informed me that he had received multiple calls from his Boeing contacts complimenting me and my team.

We worked diligently for many weeks away from home with lots of daily stress and not a lot of daily direction and support. *How things have changed.* In 2019, you would be communicating nonstop with your management seven days a week. Ultimately, my hard work and tenacity paid off and at this point, Boeing wanted to offer me a job. Simultaenously, my current employer wanted to give me a raise and promotion. This whole situation full of cumulative challenges forced me to grow up and face the world. This was definitely the hard way to get started, but it made me a stronger person. Nothing like getting thrown into the deep end of the pool without swimming lessons.

I discovered early on that I was at my best when challenged and required to present or negotiate a deal. I was effective at speaking in front of people and developing a plan. For some reason, I'm wired to want to be put up front and take the lead. I guess that's a positive trait, but I must tell you it comes with its share of pressure and commitment. I'm sure glad I had that desire and ability because if I didn't, I'm not sure what direction I would have gone in.

Thankfully, this experience gave me enough confidence to continue down the business path. It also taught me that I had more drive and ability than most of my counterparts. You will eventually see in your own experiences that challenges of this scale help teach all of us how to conquer intricate circumstances and sometimes showcase talents that you didn't know you possessed.

About a year later, I applied to the Grumman Corporation on Long Island, New York for a business management position within the Product Operations Group. This would be a major change for me since I didn't have much technical experience. I was getting frustrated with my current job and the company's management style, as well as the future outlook of the company. I received an attractive offer from Grumman and I accepted it. As often happens, my current employer presented me an offer with better perks. Fortunately, I had enough good sense to take the position with Grumman, where opportunity was abundant, and not jump at the short-term money increase.

CAUTION: Pay close attention to this lesson, since money is a tangible reward and money is instant and symbolic as status—yet there are so many more factors tied to your employment decisions and rewards come in numerous shades and colors. You can pay a high price in other areas of your life (even your sanity!) for a salary alone.

Knowing that my current employer thought I had the talent to warrant a large counter-offer gave me the needed confidence to start my new position at Grumman.

Once at Grumman, I quickly discovered that I needed to reinvent myself, meaning that I had to gain the respect of leaders and colleagues. I also had a tremendous amount to learn, as I was now working in a highly technical engineering and manufacturing environment in a business role.

My new job entailed estimating, pricing and contract negotiations involving highly sophisticated weapon systems. I dedicated myself to learn everything possible and to gain the trust and respect of a senior team.

After approximately two years, I earned a promotion to a supervisory position. I was an outsider to this group, but I impressed the management team with my work ethic, leadership skills and ability. I was also acutely aware of the fact that I needed to prove to the group that they could count on me and that I would help the organization grow and succeed. Because this was such a senior group, it had its challenges. I was strengthening my skills at a rapid pace. The management team had tremendous faith in my abilities and they were willing to take a risk with me as a junior-level leader. This was my first test at leadership and the challenge of leading senior technical personnel.

At the age of twenty-eight, I had to utilize my people skills and convince a tough group of technical experts that they should take my lead. As I will discuss further in this book, leadership and trust is earned and it is a balancing act. I slowly came to realize that I needed to make many friends in the organization while at the same time, letting the team know that I was in charge. Just because management has confidence in you doesn't mean that you will be successful. Leadership can be hard and stressful—that's why most people shy away from the responsibility. I carried my share of missteps, but fortunately, I always recovered and learned from them.

After two more years, I was promoted to a department manager position. At this point, I had sharpened my skills and I was respected by the majority of my team. My most significant accomplishment leading up to this promotion was my ability to gain the trust and respect of my team. Note that the knowledge I gained from working closely with manufacturing and engineering departments centered around the design and manufacturing of highly sophisticated tools, parts and large assemblies of military fighter jets and commercial aircraft strengthened my capabilities. This gave me the base experience of truly understanding our products from the ground floor up.

I didn't realize it at the time, but this strengthened my overall ability to become a successful business management leader and eventually, a CFO of a multi-billion-dollar division. This was not a planned career path, but it fortunately worked to my benefit. Remember: There is nothing more important to your growth path than hard work and dedication, but a little unplanned luck always helps and happens more often than you might think.

At this stage in my career, I was around thirty years old, and I was assigned to our new commercial business division. This was yet another new experience for me, as I would now be working closely with a senior management team in the pursuit of winning new business in the highly competitive commercial aircraft business.

I spent years in this aggressive, high-energy division, gaining the confidence of the president and the leadership team of the division, as well as the corporate team.

Working closely with senior business leaders in the division made me realize that I needed to elevate my broad business skills. After careful consideration, I decided to go back to college for my MBA. This was quite challenging since I had an eighteen-month-old and a brand-new infant at home. Yes, let that set in! I was a husband and new father. My wife and I decided that we could balance me going back to school. I can't stress enough how wonderful it is to have a supportive partner through this type of career trajectory; many decisions along the corporate walkway impact home life. Somehow, I completed the MBA program over the next three years at night after work. Teamwork and sacrifice enabled my wife and I to jointly make this happen. This would turn out to be a great decision for my career progression.

I was tracking on a fairly rapid career path within the Grumman Corporation and everything seemed to be on track. Then out of nowhere, the Northrop Corporation acquired the Grumman Corporation in 1994, which would change the corporate structure and culture.

Now, I needed to figure out Plan B. As you can imagine, Grumman employees were very anxious, as it usually doesn't bode well for the company that's taken over by another entity. Things started to move rapidly and I wasn't about to wait around to hear that my job was moving to California or worse, being eliminated altogether. Many of my leaders and subordinates were frozen in place, not knowing what this would mean to them personally.

I approached senior management with my concerns and they informed me that the new management team at Northrop valued me and wanted me to remain with the new company. They quickly reassigned me to a premier program that would remain in New York, at least for the foreseeable future.

That was comforting and I performed well in this new role, but I still wasn't totally convinced that I would stay in the new company.

Even though I was in a good place, I decided to search for positions in Manhattan and went to numerous interviews over the next year.

A year later, preparation and patience collided. My new director got promoted to a CFO position and out of nowhere, I was selected to replace him. In parallel, I started to receive inquiries from other companies, and I had to make a critical decision to either stay with this new company or move on to other opportunities.

My decision to earn my MBA two years earlier became even more influential, as it definitely helped me get promoted and consider other job offers. You'll come across more examples of how sacrifice, dedication and a little luck can make the difference.

I spent the next decade on a fastpaced, prestigious program in New York and gaining the respect of numerous corporate senior leaders. During this period, Northrop Grumman began to rapidly acquire several large high-tech companies, transforming it into a major defense contractor. Throughout this period of time, numerous Northrop leaders were assigned to our New York Long Island and Florida sites where I worked closely with them and gained their respect and confidence.

I was one of the few who realized the worth of reinventing yourself and pressing forward, and not dwelling on the negatives of being a "takeover victim." Invaluable lesson!

I maintained a positive attitude and I was determined to succeed, which paid off big-time for me.

In 2006, the company made a major investment in me, sending me to the Advance Management Program (AMP) at The Wharton School, where I received a university certificate and became an alumni of a formidable business school. I met senior leaders from around the world and learned from some of the finest professors and entrepreneurs of all time. This effort was a game changer for me and and helped shape the leader I became.

In 2008, I was promoted to VP and CFO of a division within the company. Now, I was really going to be tested! As evidenced by major contributions to the overall corporation's success, in 2012, I was selected in to be the VP and CFO of the company's largest division.

In 2015, the company decided to move my division headquarters to Florida where I would spend the next three years. My family remained in New York; needless to say, this required additional sacrifice for me and my family. I should also note that over the last ten years, I needed to travel to California, where our sector headquaters was located, every couple of weeks to meet with my teams assigned to the region. I was also required to attend meetings with my boss, as well as quarterly corporate reviews and other strategy meetings. I spent many days and nights on airplanes and in hotels, requiring an enormous amount of sacrifice. I mention these tidbits to keep it real and to make it clear that success has its downside.

Finally, I decided to retire from my position in November of 2017. I was still highly motivated and loaded with energy, but after ten years of constantly being away from home, made me pause and think about the next stage of my life. It's difficult to sever your ties, but I thought it was the right time to make the move and do some new things. After I took several months off from the crazy corporate life that I was living for such a long period of time, I could proceed with a clear state of mind. I loved what I did though at times, it involved deep sacrifice and significant stress.

Being a CFO granted me a seat and voice at the table with the senior leaders of the company. I believe they valued my dedication and opinions most of the time. I had a lot of influence on the company's performance and I also had the responsibility of leading numerous talented people. I knew I would miss the challenge and the people; however, I can say without hesitation, that I don't miss the stress and endless days away from my wife and kids.

So, here I am today, unwavering and convinced that I can still make a significant contribution to the business community-at-large by sharing my experiences and knowledge. Because I enjoy business and people so much, my No. 1 passion is helping future leaders.

Knowing these personal snippets, hopefully you can gauge what may have stood out in my trajectory, how I entered, how I climbed. Rather than learning one endless, boring topic, it will be the cumulative effect of multiple skills and talents that will lead to your personal greatness.

I tried to think about the type of things that molded me as a skilled worker and eventual executive. I wanted to give a view of someone who made their share of mistakes and demonstrate how you grow and mature from them. I also wanted to show how you don't necessarily have to attend a major name university to prosper.

Now that you know of my expedition, it's time to start mapping yours.

CHAPTER 2

Your Powerful Expedition: Following the 6 P's

"Do what you love and success will follow. Passion is the fuel behind a successful career"

—MEG WHITMAN

DID YOU KNOW that most of the business books out there contain twelve to fifty traits to reflect on, internalize and act on in order to be a corporate star, a purposeful leader, a top executive? Well, since you're looking to *The Brief*, let's go with...six!

Tasks and decisions on a regular daily basis can be tied to a formula of six commitments, the 6 P's.

Time can go by quickly and it's imperative that you chart your course and develop a method for monitoring your progress. It's a known fact that when you measure something, you dramatically increase the chances of success.

When reflecting on my career journey, I frequently realized that these six commitments enabled me to succeed and differentiate myself from the competition. Most of all, this formula kept me focused and determined to succeed.

Each "P" is monumental on its own, although the real power is in the understanding that collectively, the six of them offer the vision and strength required to stay focused, prepared and disciplined. When you apply the 6 P's, you will recognize the benefits they provide you towards reaching your goals.

Think about each one of these and how they can help you secure what you are striving to achieve:

◆ **Purpose.** Have a well-defined mission; goal setting.

◆ **Planning.** Establish and manage your timeline and process; stay on track. ("The only thing worse than a bad plan is no plan.")

◆ **Preparation.** Document your plan and always be ready to modify.

◆ **Priorities.** Determine the sequence of events in order of importance.

◆ **Persistence.** Formally review your status; stay relentlessly focused.

◆ **Patience.** Realize everything doesn't go according to plan and it takes time to achieve worthwhile goals and objectives; be flexible.

If you are a type-A personality like myself, this process will help you slow down and take the appropriate amount of time to plan and execute. If you are a procrastinator it will force you to document your goals and help to motivate you to stay on course.

The Brief is all about planning and measuring progress. The more progress you see yourself accomplishing, the more energy and desire you will generate for yourself, continuously stretching and growing your capabilities and marketability.

CHAPTER 3

Purpose: *Efforts and Actions*

"To become devoted to a calling, to have a sense of responsibility
and to have hopes and aspirations are all part of being human.
To have no calling, no sense of responsibility, no hopes
or aspirations, is to be outside of life."

—DR. JONAS SALK

DO YOU KNOW what your values are? What excites you? What is your talent? Do you possess any hidden gifts? Have you envisioned your life in five years or a decade? Do you have a clear portrait of your skills?

If you can answer one or all of these questions, you're in a good spot to at least consider your purpose if you've not already identified it. Sounds cliché, but ultimately, what do you wake up for? It's no surprise that Simon Sinek's book, *Start With Why*, is still a sensation after hitting the shelves and apps ten years ago! The book illustrates why living each day by being able to answer "why" energizes you to keep going, keep pushing, and contribute.

Now, for me, this drive has always come from *passion*. I suppose it's the unspoken "P" in this formula, and that's because it cannot be manufactured or nuanced. Passion is very personal. Passion is like rocket fuel. And it's not tangible for everyone. Scores of people function without passion. At the same time, efforts and actions are tangible. Efforts and actions indicate progress. Progress begets success. Success can be liberating to the point that purpose can be a grey area sometimes in the corporate world. The very *act* and *movement* of production and performance is enough to gain a position and go further.

I believe what shaped me to be a strong performer and leader throughout my career was my determination to work extremely hard and drive myself every day. Making a difference and creating some level of a legacy for others to benefit from has been the springboard for my corporate ladder. This had its upside as well as its downside. Looking back, I can now clearly evaluate the way I went about my career commitment.

From a positive standpoint, I believe one of my strongest approaches to climbing the corporate ladder was my personal commitment to learning something new every day *and* to create something new; modest or mammoth, that would strengthen my team and the overall company. Early on in my career, I was determined to be a change agent and an innovator. If you know anything about either of these nifty titles or aspirations, you know that both signal forward movement—and risk. There is no stagnancy in change or innovation. And holing up as a solitaire employee rarely breeds either!

I can't stress enough the importance and value that will

come your way if you listen, observe and carefully weigh the advice that you will get from successful leaders.

Take everyone's knowledge in, as it will be invaluable to your career journey. You will sometimes get conflicting guidance, so evaluate the advice and the right approach will present itself.

I had several mentors and each one of them displayed their own style and tactics. I valued their input and I would probably say that I took a blend of all of them and bundled it with my own personal touch. Whenever working with a senior leader, I would carefully observe their every move.

I specifically took notice with the way they would handle tough critical decisions. Working under tight deadlines in high-stress environments is the best way to see how different styles work. Watching the way they dealt with their teams under intense stress really taught me a lot.

Some of the smartest people I dealt with had no people skills and would just bully their way through the process. How quickly they lost the respect of the team of people they were leading. On the other hand, I was fortunate to work for and with some fantastic leaders who were innovators, extremely bright and incredible at leading, especially under tough circumstances.

My approach was to make sure that I stayed focused and level-headed and gave the team confidence when I found us in a stressful situation. I also realized after being in stressful situations many times through my early years of leading that panicking, yelling and losing your composure were a formula for *disaster*. Instead, you and the team need to take a breath and take a fresh look at the problem, attack it one step at a time and most of all, value the input from your team. With little exception, things will turn out well. After all, getting to the place where you are listening to others in the same professional situation *is* indicative of your efforts and actions.

The next step is to develop your path forward.

CHAPTER 4

Planning: Timeline, Process, Tracking

"There are no secrets to success. It is the result of preparation, hardwork, and learning from failure"

—COLIN POWELL

WHEN WAS THE last time you set a goal and not only accomplished it but also, accomplished it on time? Do you have a process for completing career-oriented tasks? Do you track your progress? Do you use calendars, lists or other tools to benchmark?

When starting out, I didn't view my first job out of college as the beginning of a career; I viewed it as "just a job" that return an income. I always performed well and was conscientious, but I didn't have the guidance or understanding of what it would take to *build a career*. As I matured and learned the hard way, I started to realize that I needed to push myself and get out of my comfort zone.

I inched outside the peripheral, but frankly, I didn't have clear goals and I definitely didn't have a thought-out plan. Early on, I should have studied harder and been more flexible and willing to search for opportunities and companies that would require relocation. I also would have made things a lot easier on myself if I went back for my MBA soon after I had my first position. These different approaches would have potentially opened up greater opportunities, and I firmly believe that my career path would have been accelerated.

In spite of these shortcomings, conscientiousness and intense effort every day were where I placed my priorities when I showed up for work. But I didn't necessarily plan against tasks or set goals. For instance, my way of looking at things was that I needed to be at work for eight to twelve hours every day. I would maximize that time, and not just let days and weeks pass by without making an investment and going above and beyond my daily assignments. This was my "plan!"

Don't get me wrong; there were days and probably even weeks where I lost some of that focus, but for the most part, it was the way I operated.

Do your best every day to be focused and determined to make a difference and to differentiate yourself from the masses. Those who understand that this is a "career journey" rather than "one position" will have the best chance of success. To me, it's like preparing for retirement; if you set a goal and invest every year, you will have the best chance of achieving your objectives. If you don't have goals and you don't invest every day, you will probably fall short of achieving your goal.

That being said, some people realize what it takes to succeed earlier than others. Some people get this right out of the gate and others, later on in their careers. Some never get it.

Don't let fear and anxiety get in your way and cloud your mind and freeze you in place. Like investing money for retirement, it's best when you do it early and often. Do the same with your personal career goals.

KEEPING YOUR PLAN ALIVE

When I did start devising a "living" plan—meaning, it could be flexible—the technique I used was to put things in writing. Every Monday morning, as challenging as it was starting out the week, I would quickly write down my goals and objectives for the week ahead. I would then track my progress. This was my way of ensuring that I kept my commitments and to also challenge and stretch myself. It would give me a real sense of accomplishment when I was able to see many, if not all of my weekly goals checked off at the end of the week. Naturally, there were certain weeks that I fell short of my goals.

I looked at this as my career foundation and from there, I would build from it.

Hard work meant always being there for my team and superiors.

Those who knew me well realized how much emphasis I put on being there for the team. Unfortunately, this commitment came with its share of downside. I always worked with a sense of urgency 24/7. My goal was to immediately get back to people and have a solution to every problem. My phone never got shut off and rarely did I not answer a call, text, or email within an hour. ...Truth be told, most of the time, within minutes! This was great for my team and my bosses, but it created enormous stress. I can tell you now that it was not a healthy way to live life. Don't get me wrong—I would never suggest ignoring people, especially during a potential crisis. What I am suggesting is, that you don't place every contact made to you 24/7 with the same level of urgency. You should also develop some operating guidelines, so that you don't find yourself on a path where there is never any downtime.

Use good common sense in this area, especially when it involves your boss or your boss's boss. You need to be aware of the fact that people go to those that always answer their calls, no matter what time or day it is. It's imperative that you strike a healthy balance, which is sometimes challenging.

Working with a sense of urgency and commitment is a valued trait, but it can also be taken advantage of. To a fault, I always wanted to solve problems and help where I could. I learned over time that I needed to allow for downtime, try not to get involved with every situation and pass the task off to others when appropriate. I definitely got better at this over time, but I must confess that I didn't know how to totally control my type-A personality. The important thing is to recognize that you can't be all things to all people 24/7.

Prioritize your time and put your best foot forward. Do

your best to consistently deliver superior results. You must effectively manage your time and when appropriate, take time off and enjoy yourself. For those of you who are overly driven, it's critical to find that sweet spot, balancing work and play.

Don't allow yourself to get over-subscribed, as this can create exorbitant stress and have real adverse effects on your health. When I found myself getting overwhelmed, I would take time to discuss things with a trusted co-worker or one of my mentors to get another perspective, giving me clarity and the ability to effectively deal with the stress.

Since it's hard to conceive a detailed plan when you're just starting your career, try listing what hard work means to you. Here is an example:

◆ Putting in the appropriate time at the job; never leaving things unfinished
◆ Working smartly
◆ Commitment
◆ Volunteering for special projects
◆ Finding creative solutions to problems
◆ Not waiting for the boss to ask for something (being proactive)
◆ Stretching and being resourceful
◆ Putting in long hours when required
◆ Finding ways to strengthen the performance of the group
◆ Managing/maximizing time

Is this the way you consider and work at things? I encourage you to pause and think about these actions and how you approach each one of them.

When you look at successful people, in whatever capacity that may happen to be, I can assure you that person always worked hard and was driven by a goal and a challenge.

There are no guarantees in life, but I absolutely believe that working hard to attain your dream will lead you down a positive and rewarding path. It's never a straight line, so be prepared to zig zag, as you attempt to piece the puzzle together. Stay positive and keep a smile on your face.

BRIEF STORY

What Balance?

On Christmas eve, while attending church, I received a message from a senior executive looking for me to circulate the latest year-end financial forecasts. Without hesitation, I leaned over to my wife and informed her that I needed to answer this call. Fortunately, we were there early and I had fifteen minutes to find one of my managers to see if they had an update to send me. Now, I'm involving another person into the fray and possibly ruining their evening. It didn't stop there, since I had sent out numerous inquiries to some of my finance leaders.

During the next hour, multiple people were engaged and working to get me the data. Some, on the other hand, didn't reply. Either they didn't see the message or they understandably ignored it. I am not happy to admit that I had flooded my team with my request on an important family holiday.

Within ten minutes, I had my rough answer and it would give the senior leader just enough information to ask a million more questions. I sent off the reply to my boss and went back into the church just in time for the mass to start. In my reply to my boss, I mentioned that I was "at church" and then "proceeding to a family celebration." To my surprise, my boss replied with a "thank you" and told me to "enjoy the evening." He definitely didn't take a moment to realize it was Christmas Eve until I reminded him.

I forwarded the note to my team and thanked them again and apologized for disrupting them on Christmas Eve. I was able to get myself recomposed and enjoy time with my family, although it was stressful and disruptive and I felt terrible that I didn't contact my boss before sending the action to my team. I learned that day to handle things differently in the future.

My point here is we never stop learning and recalibrating.

This happened to me many times during vacations, holidays, and other important family events...more times than I care to remember.

Finally, after many years, I realized that during these so-called "crisis calls" I needed to send a note back to whatever boss at the time was searching for me and let them know that I was attending an important event.

I would then ask them if they needed me to leave the event to take their call or action. Almost every time I did this, I was told to enjoy myself and get back to them the next day or they would contact someone else who could get them what they needed.

I didn't take the time to realize that they are human and have families and commitments and know how hard it is to deal with senior leaders looking for them during family events and commitments. There are times when you must "take the call" and do what's required. However, most of the time, you can avoid the stress and aggravation it causes everyone. At every level, you will experience moments when you need to build up some courage and talk through your concerns with your boss. You will almost always find yourself getting a positive outcome and asking yourself why you didn't have the conversation earlier. Lots of unecessary stress could be avoided.

CHAPTER 5

Preparation: *People and the Pitch*

"Talent wins games, but teamwork and intelligence
wins championships."

--MICHAEL JORDAN

HAVE YOU EVER thought of your resume as a marketing and motivational tool? Is your resume something that you are proud of at this moment? How often do you take the time to update it? Have you shown your resume to other professionals to critique it? Can you be sure that your resume reflects the target team, department, job and/or industry you're going for?

There are millions of articles out there about making sure your resume is efficient and effective. Many tips seem so simple and you may think, *wow, that is just common sense.*

The objective in this section is to mainly underscore the importance of this document and how managers truly look at them. I also want to reinforce the value they have in tracking your career progress, or in many cases, the lack of progress. Your resume is your career story and your career foundation, and it requires your proper attention. It's not for a one-time use like a pic on SnapChat. Instead, it should be a live tracking and motivational tool.

A poorly constructed resume will not be your friend. When I am speaking at universities, the students are not that interested in the format as much they are with content and strategic wording. They want my thoughts as an executive who reviews endless resumes. They want to know what will catch the attention of a potential employer. They are searching for the prompt "what do/what not to do" guidance.

Students realize that the competition is fierce, and they want to make sure they have a resume that will differentiate them. They're just not sure what will help sell them to prospective employers.

You wouldn't believe how many resumes I have seen that are not up to par, whether they're overcrowded, not clear or concise, and or even contain a crime scene of spelling mistakes grammatical errors. *Hello, spell check! Hello, spelling and grammar review!* Getting others to read your resume, looking for mistakes, is recommended.

Building and constantly enhancing your resume is vital. Constructing a resume from a blank piece of paper can be overwhelming. Whether you're a strong writer or not, you should seek professional support in creating this critical marketing tool.

Remember that your resume is your personal advertising and marketing tool and reflects who you are and what you are looking for. It is a way for you to shape and promote your credentials.

This is your opportunity to showcase yourself to current and potential employers. You should also be thinking ahead regarding your ability to keep it flexible enough, allowing you to tailor it for specific job opportunities as they present themselves. Think through the types of skills and requirements a perspective hiring manager is looking for and make sure that you showcase them on the resume. Demonstrate those specific skill requirements and highlight your proven accomplishements accordingly.

As employees are moving from job to job more frequently, having a solid resume at all times is essential. You should update your resume every quarter. I suggest adding a reminder to your calendar and allocate an hour or so to accomplish this. *Planning!* This not only ensures you have the most up-to-date resume in case a job opportunity pops up, but it also helps you to track your growth and progress.

You'll be surprised by how much you have learned and can add to your resume in this short timeframe. Make sure to highlight new skills, accomplishments, leadership experiences and projects you have been involved in. As you make these updates, remove older items and replace them with more relevant and attention-grabbing skills and accomplishments.

CAUTION: If you go six months and you cannot make your resume stronger, you are probably not growing and making yourself more marketable. Don't allow yourself to get comfortable and complacent; always stretch yourself outside of your comfort zone. Being comfortable in your job is easy, but it's not going to get you to the next step on that ladder!

Again, these are tips that may sound basic, but they are so important and impactful. You must make sure that the wording, spelling, grammar, and structure of your resume are near-perfection. I recommend having at least two others view your resume.

In terms of structure, utilize powerful and crafted bullet points. Paragraphs within resumes are usually non-effective. Remember, the goal is to capture the attention of the reader, so limited wording will effectively deliver the message. Employers normally glance at resumes quickly, usually taking about ten seconds or so; therefore, you must have things that jump off the page and hold their attention.

GO TO THE HIGHEST FLOOR: THE ELEVATOR PITCH

Whenever a resume crossed my desk, I glanced at it, focusing on the following items: one page, structure, education, school attended, GPA and key experiences and accomplishments. If it interested me, I would then take the time to read the resume much closer. The majority of the time, I would go back to the elevator summary if they had one. I think it is a good way to encapsulate in a concise manner your key attributes and goals.

I like to use the term "elevator pitch" because it has the potential to capture the attention of the prospective employer. I placed a lot of importance in getting this section of the resume right.

As with the rest of the resume, update this section frequently to be in line with your other resume updates.

There are different views on this, but I believe it is important to have a brief, but powerful summary describing your position, strengths, and goals/objectives. This should not be generic, but it should highlight who you are and what you are searching for. You need to carefully craft every word. It should set the tone for the rest of the resume.

When it comes down to it, we all have a lot to say! The real commanding skill is being able to articulate the messages in a punchy way. When you are constructing your verbal elevator pitch you can expand on this brief written summary. You should continuously modify this summary, always strengthening its content to best describe yourself. Like the rest of the resume, it's a continuous work-in-progress.

GUIDELINES FOR A POWERFUL PAGE

For building an influential resume, I recommend limiting it to one page. If there is additional information that could aid you in telling your story, construct it and have it for future reference if required. Your one-page resume should look clean to the eye in a professional format. Try putting yourself in the position of a prospective employer who is often reviewing numerous resumes in a short period of time. It must be a tool that entices the employer to want to read it. After all, would you want to read several pages of information or one well-crafted page? My answer is it should be *brief* and impactful!

It goes without saying that having strong credentials is the most significant factor in constructing a resume. Content is No. 1, but don't forget that visual appeal can make all the difference.

From there, it is critical to build your resume marketing tool with the goal of exhibiting your credentials and experiences. Never lose sight that you will be competing with other comparable candidates, so think through ways that will differentiate you from the competition.

Just like any other product packaging tool, it can either sell you or pop your resume in the trash. You've worked hard to develop and build a portfolio of skills and accomplishments, and you now need to make sure that you spend the appropriate time and energy required to make your marketing tool of the highest quality.

Place the *summary* "elevator pitch" right up front at the top of the page, followed by your education and GPA. If you are proud of your college and your grades, highlight them next. From there, assemble a list of key skills and accomplishments in order of importance. You know you are in a good place if you have too many items to choose from! You will get many opinions on this, but I always wanted to see how a prospective employee could elevate their skills and accomplishments in three or four sentences. As an executive, I valued this ability in my staff in all aspects of business, including when they were presenting to me or my leadership.

Once you have what you consider a professional-caliber product, obtain a couple of opinions from mentors, coaches or expert resume consultants. It can sometimes get a little confusing with multiple opinions, but it's valuable and insightful to get different perspectives. Like most critical decisions, you will need to weigh all the input and make an informed decision on how to proceed.

When it comes to the *experience* section of the resume, I'm a big proponent of using concise, impactful bullet points to deliver the message. I am not a fan of reading a litany of short paragraphs. Frankly, I usually pushed those resumes to the side. Once again, I would be searching for an individual who understood the value of being able to elevate their story in a precise manner.

Once you land the interview (yeah!), there will be plenty of opportunities to verbally embellish your points. The No. 1 goal is finding a way to get the prospective employer to read most (if not all) of your resume without being bored to tears, or worse, turned off by the way it looks.

Simple, focused bullet points will enable the reader to rapidly understand your experience and capabilities. Being able to keep the bullets simple with clarity is critical. The reality is that most managers are reading these resumes in between meetings or during other times where they aren't as focused as one might think they *should* be.

Knowing this can often be the case, it's imperative that you understand the importance of brevity, but not at the expense of content. If the readers are intrigued, they will go back at another time in their day or even week and reexamine your resume with a more focused intent.

When constructing these bullet points, first get your thoughts down on paper. They will usually be much too long, but you need to start with lots of content to choose from. Then you can mature these bullet points until you are satisfied that they tell your full story. Limit each to one or two lines. Make sure that you spend the proper amount of time selecting action words like *led, managed, accomplished, created, selected*.

You only have one page, so you will need to select the most impactful points to make your compelling case. You should prioritize them and place them in that order. It's all about making sure the prospective employer reads as much as possible without losing interest. Choose four or five accomplishment bullet points and four or five specific skill sets for your most recent job experience. If you think it's essential to add another previous job or two, be sure to limit the content to two or three bullet points.

Focus on selecting skills or experiences that may be different or that complement those that are included in your current position. This is also a good way to demonstrate your career and *skill progression*. If you are coming straight out of college, you should use your internship experiences.

There is often a tendency for most people to jam in way too much information onto the resume. This forces you to use a font that is usually making the document unreadable. It also signals to the reader that you didn't think this through, you are not capable of prioritizing your thoughts and you lack the written communication and possibly the verbal skills the position requires.

In a matter of a few seconds, these thoughts cross the mind of the reader and they push the resume to the side. You could have great credentials that never get viewed because of your inability to effectively construct your resume.

Make sure you aren't using acronyms, buzz words, abbreviations, "I" or "me". The wording of each bullet point requires thoughtfulness and creativity. Each should be carefully written and scrutinized. You will be pleasantly surprised how effective these well-crafted bullet points can be!

Within the *skills* section, you want to ensure that you are using terminology, professional systems/tools and experiences that the potential employer will be looking for. The reader will be searching for things that catch their eye. Tailor the wording to effectively align to the potential employer's needs. I must emphasize that this doesn't mean adding skills that you don't have; it means shape the words to best illuminate the skill and your degree of expertise. Honesty and integrity can never be compromised. For the resume to do its intended use will likely require you to tweak depending on the specific job you are targeting.

The next section should depict your key *accomplishments*.

These bullet points need to demonstrate how you have utilized your skills and talents as they relate to the requirements of the position you are pursuing. Prospective employers will be looking for talent that will help them strengthen their organization and the overall company. Selling your skills and accomplishments require more than just assembling a laundry list of items. The skills section is obviously important, but the accomplishment section solidifies the points to the reader that you have some level of a proven track record, whether you are straight out of college or someone with several years of business experience. The objective is to demonstrate that you are resourceful, creative, and strategic, possess some level of leadership skills and have strong communication skills.

Craft your unique story. Make sure there is continuity throughout the entire resume.

Once you have selected your top accomplishment bullet points, you, take the time to finess the info with key action words to emphasize your points. Examples include:

- developed
- exceptional
- implemented
- accountable
- completed
- motivated
- selected
- urgency
- generated
- focused
- responsible

Other key information to include on the resume:

- scholarships
- internships
- honors/awards
- computer technology skills
- community service
- foreign language skills
- leadership examples

Make sure that you select things that bring value to the job you are pursuing.

CAUTION: Do not to use buzz words or phrases like *team player, conscientious worker,* or *loyal employee.* These are the types of things that are expected. Don't use valuable space stating something that is expected. In addition, don't furnish personal information on the resume such as age/birthdate, marital status, religion, political affiliation, or your picture (head shot). You want to keep the resume non-controversial. I would also recommend that you stay away from controversial subjects during the interview process as well.

As you can see, there are many critical factors to know when constructing a powerful professional resume. It may require multiple iterations to get it to a place where you feel you have a resume that you can be proud of and most of all, one that will do the job of landing you the job!

This is your pathway to securing an interview. Continue to strengthen your resume on a regular basis. As I was striving to advance myself up through the ranks of leadership, I would continuously challenge myself by adding/modifying bullet points on my resume for things that I needed to accomplish if I was going to continue to grow and mature. I would highlight these items in a red font and put a plan together, along with a timeline for accomplishing these new goals.

This was a method for me to visually see what I needed to do going forward and how much more marketable I would be with them.

Whenever I went back to modify my resume, I would see these red bullets staring me in the face. Quite often, I realized that I made little to no progress on some of them. This would force me to reflect and frankly, push me to deal with my inability to achieve my goals.

Using your resume as a motivational tool makes you pause and think about what you must do to climb to the next level. This technique ussually forced me to take stock and push me to get my act toghether. Give it a try!

A colleague and I would often review each other's resumes and give honest critiques. You almost need to make it a game and try to keep stretching yourself. I give this perspective to demonstrate that this is a competitive never-ending journey.

The people who are highly motivated are usually the ones that regularly seek my advice regarding the almighty resume. Starting from a blank sheet of paper is challenging at first. Once you populate the resume, it becomes a lot easier to mature and finesse. Remember, you must have the credentials, but you must also be able to effectively and efficiently market those hard-earned credentials.

Don't allow yourself to get stagnant and lulled into believing your credentials and resume are the best. Time passes quickly and you will get caught up in the daily grind.

LIVING UP TO YOUR RESUME

Once you have a resume that you can be proud of, you can get ready for the interviewing process that lies ahead. *Prepare, prepare, prepare.* This is your time to effectively communicate your qualifications, unique capabilities and the powerful reasons why you would be a good fit with the interviewing company. This can be daunting, especially for someone with little to no interviewing experience and training. Practice with people who will give you honest and constructive feedback and guidance. To some degree, you will can think of this as an audition. You must know what you're doing and be prepared. Do not think that you are good on your feet and you can just "wing it." I can assure you that this could be catastrophic to your career before it progresses.

Not only should you have your talking points well-thought out; you must practice your delivery. Don't let yourself get lulled into thinking that you know what you're doing and practice isn't required. By being prepared it will help give you the confidence and calmness needed to articulate the answers to many difficult sets of questions by the interviewer(s). They will be able to get a sense if you are serious and prepared for them.

It will be essential to be prepared when answering questions and let the interviewer know that you are well-versed in the company's products, leadership team and operating culture. This is where you want to fluidly deliver your elevator pitch. You should have a short and long version. It is easy for an interviewer to trip you up with even a simple question like, "Tell me about yourself." So many people go blank when asked this somewhat simple but potent question!

I would always ask interviewees to tell me a little about themselves to kick things off. It's incredible just how much information an individual will divulge when asked this question. This response sets the tone for the rest of the interview process. When asked this question, you must be prepared to supply a thoughtful response.

Always be honest and genuine. Make sure that you don't allow yourself to drift, giving way more information than required. I've had some very bright people tell me way too much and unfortunately, expose glaring weaknesses. In this situation, "less is more". It was a great way for me to flush out things that I would have never learned through the traditional interviewing-questioning process.

When preparing, use a mirror and/or video yourself. Attend mock interview practice training sessions. It can sometimes be quite painful to watch, but the benefits are invaluable. It's much better to screw things up in practice instead of during an important real-world interview. Unfortunately, most people do not practice and they experience a real catastrophe that could have been avoided.

I continue to coach people preparing for important interviews. I can't think of a time in which the participant didn't thank me and tell me how much they didn't know when it came to the interviewing process. The ones that seek advice are usually the ones who take the process seriously and are looking for ways to enhance their chances of success.

At the same time, I always make sure that I underscore the importance of not getting bogged down with too much information, which can start to cloud your head with too much stuff. Most of all, be calm, natural and upbeat.

I encourage finding as many people as possible to get a good inside perspective of the company. Do extensive research regarding the executive leadership team, the company's key product lines, as well as company culture. Sometimes this information is obscure online. Dig deep. Can you find someone to message on LinkedIn? Can you check out reviews on Career Builder or Indeed?

You should be prepared to answer standard-type questions. Anticipate these questions and develop strong, appropriate responses. You can't think of every possible question, but you can prepare for a lot of them.

Below are a few of the do's and don'ts for successful interviewing. Some are basic, but you would be surprised how many times they are overlooked, causing a disastrous outcome.

Do

◆ Dress in appropriate attire.

◆ Be well-groomed.

◆ Be on time (or ten minutes early).

◆ Be energetic and enthusiastic.

◆ Display/project confidence.

◆ Try to stay calm and composed.

◆ Be respectful.

◆ Listen carefully to the interviewer's questions before you respond.

◆ Don't be overanxious.

◆ Have a firm and respectful handshake.

◆ Keep your hands folded on the table.

◆ Sit up straight and slightly forward.

Don't

◆ Never lie.

◆ Don't stretch the truth.

◆ Don't answer cell phones calls; make sure phone is on silent or leave outside the room.

◆ Avoid controversial topics (politics, religion, etc.).

◆ Don't oversell yourself.

◆ Don't ask about salary, vacation, bonuses, etc.

◆ Don't slump back in your seat, looking too relaxed, uninterested and overly confident.

QUESTIONS TO EXPECT

1. What has been your most recent rewarding accomplishment?

2. Are you more energized by working with data or collaborating with others?

3. How would you describe yourself in terms of your ability to work as a member of a team?

4. What motivates you to put forth your greatest effort?

5. What are your strengths? Weaknesses?

6. What influenced you to choose this career?

7. What near-term specific goals have you established for your career?

8. Given the investment the company will make in hiring and training you, can you give us a reason to hire you?

9. Would you describe yourself as goal driven?

10. What short-term goals and objectives have you established for yourself?

11. Can you describe your long-term goals and objectives?

12. How would you evaluate your ability to deal with conflict?

13. Why did you decide to seek a position in our company?

14. Do you have a geographic preference?

15. Would it be a problem to relocate?

16. To what extent are you will to travel for the job?

17. How do you differentiate yourself from other candidates?

18. How has your college experience prepared you for business career?

19. Tell me what you know about our company.

PEOPLE AND THE PITCH
DELUXE—SECRET TIPS

There are some things that you just can't prepare for. They can make a big difference in the final outcome. Be a good listener. Many interviewers will talk about themselves and you should pick up on things that may help you connect with them, such as common interests. Sometimes you can pick up a point about the interviewer that will enable you to find common interests with you, like: golfing, skiing, boating, tennis, cooking, gardening, etc. This can sometimes turn into a real ice breaker. It's not something that you can predict, but if the opportunity arises, try to use it to your benefit.

People looking to hire someone are obviously searching for highly talented, educated people with strong experience, but never underestimate the value of common interests as a discriminator. When interviewers have to make their final decision and it's a close call between several candidates, "likeability" usually seals the deal. Every situation is unique and when in doubt, go with your instincts.

It has now become common for there to be multiple interviewers participating from different organizations and it almost always has a human resources representative on the team. Things get more interesting when there are multiple people conducting the interview. Just remember that you can't be all things to all people. However, the bonus of this type of panel interview is that you get rare insight into the company's "collective personality" by touching several individual personalities. Instead of letting the group atmosphere overwhelm you, address each person by making eye contact and repeating their names. Observe! Who smiles warmly? Who's looking at her phone? Who takes the lead in asking the questions? How is everyone dressed?

Be genuine; they will pick up on that quality. When a group of interviewers evaluate you, it will be imperative that they all believe that you will be a good fit in the organization.

Whenever I was on an interviewing panel, the output from the panel would usually consist of the following criteria:

◆   Technical skills
◆   Education (school and grades)
◆   Overall resume content and professionalism
◆   Internship and other real-world experiences
◆   Previous employment
◆   Composure and presence

Most often, the human resources group will do a good job screening the applicant and the panel has had time to digest their credentials prior to the formal interview session. More times than not, the panel will get through the more typical interview questions to validate what is on your resume and to get a little more detail regarding the interviewee's skills and experience. Once those things are accomplished the questioning will get a little more fluid in order to get to know more about the applicant and gain a great sense of their goals and objectives. A team of interviewers will also probe candidates in pursuit of flushing out more potential positive qualities and potential shortcomings that will cause the company to potentially pass on them.

Some interviewers are quite skilled at the interviewing process whereas others fall short and would rather not be there, which can sometimes make the experience seem unorganized and confusing.

Keep your cool, remain polite and stay focused, especially when you get a "stupid" question. Never lose your composure even if you feel that one of the interviewers is not in your court. When the panel convenes they will all listen to each other's thoughts and opinions. It almost always comes down to one or two of the key players who will get their way. The hiring manager is obviously the No. 1 person to win over. The other participants will likely weigh in concerning your soft skills more than the job's desired technical skills. They are all important and you need to be mindful of that throughout the interview process.

After you have validated your technical skills, be prepared to successfully sell these additional skills and capabilities. If it's close between two or three candidates, it will most often come down to specific discriminators. Ask yourself how you would articulate your abilities regarding these items:

◆ Presence and composure. You want the interviewer(s) to come away with the opinion that you stood out from the pack and that you were calm, confident and sincere. This is an indicator that you will be able to handle stress and adversity.

◆ Overall communication skills. Being able to clearly articulate your thoughts in a manner that conveys confidence and not rambling on with your answers is an art and science. Ensure that you are able to consolidate your responses and questions so they are clear and concise. People tend to give long answers and they find themselves repeating and sometimes mixing up the message, leaving the interviewer confused and bored. You are not there to entertain (unless this is your skillset); however, you are there to prove that you can represent the company and start out being an individual contributor. Brevity and clarity is key—with your personality sprinkled in. The more you say, the greater the chance that you will say something that will adversely affect your chances of success. Keep in mind that "less is more". The interviewers will be accessing your ability to frame and deliver your answers. Sit straight up in the chair and look each interviewer in the eyes when answering their questions. Don't lean back in the chair giving the interviewers the sense that you are over relaxed. Conversely, don't lean too much in the forward direction giving the impression of being overly aggressive. Keep your hands calmly positioned on top of the table.

◆ **Leadership qualities**. Demonstrate that you are a proven leader in whatever capacity that may be. Make sure you find a way to integrate this into the interview process and discussions. Managers are looking for employees that are self-starters and ready to take on a challenge. Giving the interviewers the confidence that you are resourceful and able to hit the ground running is a big selling point in today's fast-paced business environment. If you are interviewing for a management position, be prepared to have several powerful leadership examples that you can fluidly pass onto them.

◆ **Adaptability.** Having the ability to seamlessly adapt to changing conditions gives the management team confidence that you are able to shift gears quickly and learn and execute new things. It is also important that you convince them that your aperture is wide open and that you are willing and able to calmly and effectively deal with adversity.

◆ **Agility.** Leadership will be searching for individuals who can operate in a demanding everchanging environment and able to fluidly work with numerous leaders on short notice without a lot of hand holding. Today's workforce is made up of many cultural and generational groups that require individuals to understand that there are obvious differences in thought and approaches. It's imperative that you give the interviewers the confidence that you can work effectively with others and that you understand and value the benefits of a diverse workforce.

◆ **Accountability.** Taking responsibility for your work and your actions is a really big deal. Give the interviewers a good sense that you know what you need to do to grow your skills and what you need to do to support the goals/performance of the business. Your mission is to have them come away from the interview saying that you understand the importance of commitment and accountability. Be cognizant that they are looking for new hires that will make their jobs easier and strengthen the results of the organization. Demonstrate that you take your position seriously and that you take responsibility for your actions and the quality of your work and that you have unwavering ethics.

◆ **Resourcefulness.** Being able to get information and summarize data with potential solutions is a welcomed and valuable asset to the hiring manager. Emphasize the point that you understand the importance and value of bringing solutions to the leader, versus continuous problems. A can-do attitude will leave a positive impression.

◆ **Creativity and innovativeness.** This is an area where you need to segway from the technical skills as they pertain to the day-to-day responsibilities of the position. Giving the impression that you are inquisitive and that you want to drive change and improvement into the processes and systems shows that you are able to perform your daily projects and are capable of making a difference to the successful results of the company and its profitability. Leaders are not looking for "robots". They require creative thinkers who are capable of creating and driving positive forward thinking and results. Demonstrate to the interviewers that you have a record of driving innovative change that streamlines the operation and enables a more efficient/effective set of processes. This again will help differentiate you from the competition. Be prepared to give examples of your successes. Underscore the value you always place on quality and the goal of driving for perfection.

◆ **Strategic.** Beyond being a change agent, demonstrate to the interviewers that you have the ability to think strategically, versus someone who just gets the job done as directed. You have the ability to think through problems and minimize or eliminate roadblocks. Come up with ways to articulate the value you put on being strategic and the importance of thinking about the future of the business.

◆ **Likeability.** Be personable and engaging. Being a suitable fit with the hiring organization personality-wise cannot be overstated, but there is no boilerplate for this. It must come from your ability to connect.

———————————

When the interview comes to an end, approach each one of the interviewers, firmly shake their hand and thank them for their time and consideration. In addition, be ready for the interviewers(s) to continue the conversation in a much less formal manner. This can often be a good sign. Take their lead and if they just want to chat be sure that you are aware that they could just be trying to get another final feel about you as a person.

If you find yourself in this position, stay calm and professional, and don't drift off doing and saying things that you wouldn't do in the formal setting. Also, count on your instincts; this is where being good on your feet really becomes a plus.

The more interviews you go on, the better prepared you will be when the right opportunity presents itself. *Practice, practice, practice.* Remember, image is critical—don't act or lie, and be clear, authentic and confident.

Several hours later, send an email to each one of the interviewers with a thank-you note. If you don't get a card from each of them, ask the leader or the human resources person for the company contact information. I recommend constructing the framework of the note the day before the interview so you can give it the proper thought. After the interview, you can embellish with some key items that you learned during the interview or something that you want to reinforce; or if necessary, adding additional clarity. Keep it simple and upbeat. Check spelling and grammar. You may also want to get advice from your mentor before hitting the send button. I always enjoyed getting a positive email at the end of a long, hard day.

These are a few items you should consider including in your email:

- ◆ "It was a pleasure meeting you and the entire panel."
- ◆ "I'm excited about the potential opportunity to join your team."
- ◆ "Are there any additional questions or information that you require?"
- ◆ "Thank you for time and consideration."

THE COLLECTION
(OF SOCIAL, AMBITIOUS PEOPLE)
—NETWORKING

How succesful are your networking skills? Do you believe networking opens doors? Can you give examples where networking worked for you?

Effective networking isnt a result of luck. It requires hard work and persistence. Networking is a critical concept to understand, embrace and use in your daily lives. Effective networking skills is a valuable tool and can have a forceful multiplying effect when it comes to meeting new people and securing new connections. It can sometimes require a person to step out of their comfort zone. There are simple methods to start up a conversation and to explore potential unknown opportunities. I'm always pleasantly surprised every time I start up a conversation with someone that I never met before, only to find out that they know someone I know or some other connection. Most people will share many things in a quick, passing conversation. In a very short period of time, some people will tell you what they do for a profession and try to see if you know people that they may know. I've also been given business cards and that really helps solidify the contact and enable a potential follow-up with that person.

Most people want to help others and will try to find a way to help another person make connections to others. Individuals that I mentor will frequently ask me how I start up cold conversations. I tell them that I often just look to see if a person is wearing a shirt or hat with a company logo, or college, town, local sports team name on it that can aid me in striking up a conversation. I find that the best time to talk to people are when you are in a line at the bank, deli, etc. If I don't have a specific lead in hint I will just find some other way to strike up a conversation.

If the individual has an outgoing personality, it becomes quite easy. Once the conversation starts to flow, I usually try to find commonality between us and play on it from there. This will come easy for some and for others, it will take practice. By no means am I suggesting that you just stop and talk to every person you come in contact with. What I am suggesting is that you need to rely on your instincts when deciding who and when to reach out to total strangers. It is important that you be aware of your surroundings and the potential new contacts that you will run into in your daily lives.

Within the power of networking, it is necessary to be prepared for the new contact you will meet. As mentioned in Chapter 5, create and memorize a verbal elevator pitch. When someone asks you what you do for a living or what your current skills, interests, or goals are, you want to seamlessly give them a response. Trying to formulate these thoughts on the fly usually causes most people to get a little flustered and ultimately fail in conveying their abilities and desires. With practice, you will be able to appear very natural and professional. This will become your personal advertising tool.

These are a few items that you should consider when constructing your fluid elevator talking points:

◆ College attended
◆ Degree
◆ Current employer
◆ Major skills
◆ Future goals

Conversations with strangers can be invigorating and inspiring. At the same time, it helps to have a networking plan. *Planning!* As a matter of fact, because networking can trip up professionals at all levels to the point of avoiding it altogether, I will venture out and suggest that networking applies all 6 P's. For beginners, *patience* may be at the top. For experts, *purpose* may be at the top, particularly if they value making a difference, leading by example and serving others. A "network" is never solo.

Here is a standard networking plan that works at all levels:

◆ Search out influential mentors.

◆ Utilize internet technology.

◆ Carefully use social media such as Facebook, Instagram and Twitter.

◆ Frequently leverage LinkedIn, spanning the contact list and newsfeed (contributing and commenting) at minimum.

◆ Let people know that you are in the job market search process.

◆ Conduct informal interviews.

◆ Create a list of potential contacts.

◆ Create a business card.

◆ Keep a log of contacts (status and dates).

◆ Conduct circular follow-ups.

◆ Talk to professors, career services, alumni, current employers and volunteer groups, internships, neighbors, relatives, club members, and church members.

◆ Once you have made the contact, maximize the situation by asking if there is anything you can do for them, don't be timid, strive to make an impression, manage the conversation by 80% listening and 20% talking.

When contacts ask you about yourself regarding your education, goals and pursuits, be prepared to respond with a fluid reply that succinctly tells your story. Developing that thirty-second, high-level set of talking points and using it in cold connections will provide you with good practice for when you get asked from a potential employer to tell them a little about yourself. Of course, you want to tweak this elevator speech depending on the opportunity and the person you are meeting with. The big message here is be prepared for all opportunities. With practice, this should roll right off your tongue sounding very authentic.

Since I have an outgoing personality, it's relatively easy for me to meet new people. I am also relatively good on my feet, though I quickly found out years ago that I did not have an instant, brief response.

That's when I realized that I needed to be more prepared and give a new contact information that they could understand while not boring them to sleep. I also made sure that I was upbeat and that they would want to continue the conversation. Having a friendly personality goes a long way. It should also be noted that you need to be a good listener. Tons of great information can come from total strangers and most individuals want to tell you about themselves.

I have encountered countless senior corporate executives, private business owners, and politicians at weddings, barbeques, and restaurants, and on vacation. Most people, and specifically executives and those in influential leadership positions, are willing to speak with you and to offer some level of help in your pursuits. Sometimes it's as simple as just asking for assistance. It's amazing how much people will tell you about themselves. Politely listen to their story and then at the appropriate time, convey your current situation through a version of your elevator statement. Then wait for them to respond, and they may be willing to lend you support. You just never know when that magical encounter will take place.

The percentage of meeting people that are willing and able to help you may be greater than you may think. The more comfortable you are in reaching out to people, the better you will get at it and the greater the chance of networking becoming your newfound method of promoting yourself. Once you see how beneficial networking is, you will experience its value.

A business card should accompany every conversation you have, which means you should carry a few with you at all times. Always ask for theirs in exchange, and if they don't have one, offer to add their contact info to your phone. Make sure you firmly shake their hand and thank them for taking the time and interest in helping you. Follow up a couple of days later with a text or email thanking them for their time. If your intuition kicks in, ask for their advice or if they can help you make a contact with someone they may know. You should also send them a resume so they can be more familiar with your qualifications.

Whether actions ensues from the initial contact or their acquaintance, it can take time. There are no guarantees that these contacts will turn into an opportunity of any kind, but a network is a playing field for any and every possibility. Don't get discouraged. If nothing else, networking gives you excellent practice for formal interviews. I am a firm believer that the more you're out there promoting yourself, the greater the chances of success.

Another networking tip is to contact professors, friends, neighbors, and relatives and see how they can help you regarding your career pursuits. Send them your resume and a short note resembling your verbal elevator speech, so they are clear with your credentials and goals and it gives them a synopsis to describe you when they reach out to their contacts. Thank them for their help, ask if there is any way you can be of service to them and follow up in the future for updates. Once again, you will be pleasantly surprised how much people want to help. Be cognizant of the fact that they are probably consumed with their own daily lives, so any lapse requires you to delicately and professionally refresh their memory regarding the support they offered you.

You can also search for them on LinkedIn to get additional insight. Sometimes you might even find that they have a common friend or business acquaintance to you.

There are so many examples that I have experienced where one contact morphs into multiple connections.

Once you experience this for yourself, you'll gradually become a pro! With the aid of the Internet, endless information is at your fingertips. Scrutinize everything that you are putting out on social media. It is a great way to connect to large numbers of people...globally. Be smart about the information you are putting out there. Social media can be an incredible networking tool regarding your future endeavors, but on the flip side, it can also do irreputable damage to your reputation and career goals if not used with the highest level of professionalism and ethics. That being said, capitalize on this connection tool; the more knowledge and contacts you have the greater the odds of landing a great opportunity.

In parallel, you should be working with recruiters and career placement groups in your college. It's very beneficial to meet with these individuals face to face. You are your best promoter and you need to make the effort to spend some time with these contacts so you can passionately make your sales pitch. More practice for the real job interviews. You need to be *persistent* and *patient* at the same time. The more people you meet, the larger your sphere of opportunity becomes.

It's amazing how many people will contact me looking for help in finding a new position. They usually start out by expressing that they feel "odd" asking me for help. I, like many others, am usually very willing to try and help someone, especially if they are having a difficult time with the whole job searching process. I try to put the person at ease. I'm also very frank with them, letting them know that they need to be patient and proactive and try to minimize the stress they are experiencing associated with this sometimes frustrating job searching process. Once we get that out of the way, I ask them for highlights regarding their skills, experience and recent employment.

More times than not, I need to recalibrate them and attempt to get them focused by clearing their heads from all the frustration they may be experiencing.

At this point, I try to summarize the information they have given me and I make suggestions on how they can condense the information into an elevator pitch.

I also ask them an assortment of questions so I have a better idea on what they're searching for, their willingness to relocate and what interviews, if any, they've been on to-date. I inquire if they have received feedback from interviews. Once I have this information I am better suited to think of people I know who could potentially help them or point them in the right direction. My main objective is to align them with people that I believe could be helpful in their search. This is where the networking connections start to take shape. I will give them names of people to contact, with permission to use my name as a reference when trying to make contact. I will often contact people directly if I think they would rather hear from me than the person I'm trying to help.

It's like being in sales. You must work at this every day and be well-prepared, determined, upbeat and eventually, the big opportunity will hit. You must remember that this is your job and it's critical that you stay focused on your goal. I've often witnessed where a person becomes frustrated and disheartened and then two or three opportunities pop up within days of each other. I can't tell a person how long it will take to find a job, but I can reinsure them that they will eventually achieve their goal and things will miraculously take shape if they stay the course.

I always emphasize the value of networking and do my level best to make them a believer: "Instead of better glasses, your network gives you better eyes!" It's like having mini-agents out there working on your behalf.

Networking is also invaluable when navigating your career through the corporate environment. I suggest that you meet and gain exposure with as many people inside the company as possible and ask others to introduce you to all levels of the organization.

One of the many things I did for my mentees was make a call to peers or to my leadership, asking them if they would be willing to spend time with my mentee to offer exposure to senior leaders. I can't think of a time that they didn't accommodate my request. Frequently, they gave my mentee more time and information than they requested. Personally, I was always willing to take the time and effort to speak with employees and support them in any way I could. Leaders are usually more than happy to help others. You just need to find the right person to assist you in making the contacts. The majority of people will never reach out like this because they are, understandably, intimidated by the thought of reaching out to leadership.

I'm passing this information onto you so you can realize how feasible it is to open doors that most will never knock on.

The big secret is leaders love to feel important and they cherish the ability to use their status and influence to help junior members. Reach out and I am confident that you will find out how approachable leaders are and their willingness to help you.

Networking is magical. Become a believer and it will serve you well.

BRIEF STORY

Contacts with Lifelong Rewards

I went from a state of cluelessness on how to publish a book to making contacts that would help me get from a concept in my head, to the words tumbling out on the pages, and sharing *The Brief* with a network I've recently cultivated.

My daughter introduced me to a private business owner who also wrote a couple of books and is involved with public speaking. He had delivered the commencement speech at her MBA university graduation.

I met with him and he offered an abundance of valuable guidance. From that point, he introduced me to his editor, a two-time Pulitzer Prize winner, who gave me some tough love and further guidance. I was encouraged that he read the entire manuscript even though he was fully engaged for the next year and couldn't work with me. Believing it served as a positive message, he also motivated me to continue to pursue the launch of my book. He believed it served a very positive and much needed message.

I went on LinkedIn and searched for highly qualified editors. To my surprise, I received a significant number of interested highly qualified writers. After careful consideration, I selected my current editor. Great decision!

Next, my editor put me in contact with a cover designer.

In parallel, I joined social networking (Facebook and Instagram) and began to put more emphasis on my existing LinkedIn network. As of this writing, I have 1,400+ contacts and I'm adding more every day. I've also requested close family members and friends to use their network of contacts, using these platforms to cast a much larger net, as I get ready to the launch the book. I'm targeting 10,000 contacts involving all age groups and diversity. As I continued to talk up and promote my book prior to its release, many friends and family members were offering to promote the book on their social media platforms. *The Brief* actually took on its own life. That indicated people liked and valued the content in the real world approach to the guidance and tips for early career success.

And there's more!

While working on these initiatives, my accountant told me during my tax return visit that he had a client who owns a media company. After more discussion, he introduced me to her. I reached out to her and she was very willing to share professional advice and connect me with a company that partners with speakers involving the type of engagements I will be pursuing. She continued to ask for updates regarding the book and speaking engagements and continued to give me her professional guidance.

Make no mistake—this all happened within a few months of networking and utilizing the 6 P's. The hardest "P" for me was *patience*!

Another networking example is when my family was at a lively birthday party at a restaurant. At the bar, I began to strike up a conversation with a good friend of the person we were celebrating. It turns out that he went to the same university as my daughter. Opitmizing that information, I asked when he graduated and where he was working. By the time we finished our drink, I had a wealth of information and many areas of commonality. I then asked my son and daughter to join us. With the university in common, it was an easy introduction.

This new acquaintance, a senior financial managing director for a financial institution in Manhattan, agreed to help my son, who was seeking a position at a similar company. He gave my son his contact information and said he would try to help him make some good contacts. Then he mentioned that his college roommate had a prominent position in this field at one of the big banks and he would find a way to connect them.

A couple of days later, they met in person. His guidance helped my son tremendously, as he made his way into the banking industry, where he currently works for the largest bank in the world. In this instance, the contact didn't directly get him his next opportunity, but he did give him perspective and valuable guidance. It also enabled him to expand his network with another major player.

CHAPTER 6

Priorities: Job Search and Selection

"Be humble. Be hungry. And always be the hardest
worker in the room."

—DWAYNE "THE ROCK" JOHNSON

WHAT DO YOU want from your career? Do you want to stay
in your current location or relocate? What are you willing to be
flexible about? What benefits are most important to you? Are
your salary expectations based on researching the market and
knowing what others are making in comparable positions? Do
you have a preferred work style?

I recently read a quote from an executive searching for a
new position. I think it pertains to anyone seeking a professional position. "Waiting for the right position with the right
company is the right thing to do."

As a recent grad searching for your first full-time position,
focus on the type of industry you're interested in, the company's
culture and employee benefits. It's common for new hires to
put the majority of their focus on the salary opportunities.

This is obviously an important item as you want to maximize your earning power after all of your college commitment and expenses. That said, my advice is to start with what I think is the most important decision: choosing the right type of industry and specific job that will best fulfill your passion and objectives.

Compensation is obviously important, but it shouldn't be at the expense of doing something that really doesn't interest you. Being happy and satisfied with the work you will be doing will make all the difference.

In terms of your first job search, if you were fortunate enough to have had a terrific internship you can make a more informed decision since you were an insider and already know a lot about the company. That's one of the many reasons why I think internships are so valuable; you know the company and the company knows you. It takes the mystery out of the decision. Even if you don't choose the company you interned for, it at least gives you the experience of knowing what to look for in a company and manager so you have a better chance of not being blindsided.

I always made a point of telling people that I interviewed that this is a big decision for both parties. Neither one of us wants to make a bad decision, since both of us will ultimately be investing a lot of time and money. I would make the analogy that choosing a company is like a marriage; making a mistake is both emotional and costly!

Most of the time, early career searchers desperately want that first job and are willing to jump at the first opportunity that comes their way.

CAUTION: Weigh all criteria involving this big decision. Don't be afraid to ask follow-up questions post-offer. What kind of schedule will be expected, or is the position solely based on results? Do you know how many company holidays, sick days and vacation days come with your initial package? Has there been any discussion on company policies that may be unique to your position or the industry as a whole? These are just a few examples of things that may be obscure until weeks into the job.

If you have a business degree you should think about some of the following types of jobs. Try to talk to people who have positions in these disciplines and see if this type of work they are performing would interest you:

- Finance
- Accounting
- Communications and Marketing
- Analytical Research (or BI, Business Intelligence)
- Operations
- Procurement
- Contracts
- Risk Management
- Sales
- Mergers and Acquistions
- Investment Banking
- Stock/Bond Trader

Industries

◆ Defense

◆ Pharmaceutical

◆ Banking

◆ Stock Exchange

◆ Consulting

◆ Environmental

◆ Software

◆ Computer Technology

◆ Entertainment

◆ Energy

◆ Medical

Other Considerations

◆ Company culture

◆ Executive leadership

◆ Medical benefits

◆ 401K savings plan

◆ Profit sharing program

◆ Probation period

◆ Graduate school reimbursement programs

◆ Career growth opportunities

◆ Training programs

◆ Logistics (mass transit options)

◆ Area housing options and costs

This is a shopping list of things you will need to consider. More than likely, you will not be able to achieve them all. Prioritize your requirements and try to remember that the beginning of your career story is about making an informed decision and balancing what's most important to you at this time in your life. Hopefully, you can see why "compensation" is just one ingredient involved in making this big decision.

There will most likely be some things that will require you to compromise on, as nothing is 100% "perfect." (Notice, a "P" that I stay away from as guidance!)

Keep your priorities straight and things will work out. If you are convinced that you will be working for a good leader and a reputable company with strong ethics and an open and positive culture. move forward.

Let's take a little deeper look at these considerations.

COMPANY CULTURE

Depending on your personality, you should attempt to find a match with a company that makes you feel comfortable yet energized and challenged. Some companies spend a great deal of time and energy making sure that they have a highly engaged workforce and they value the opinions and recommendations of their employees. In other companies, they may not place nearly the amount of focus and funding needed to measure and support employees' needs and desires. You can usually get a good sense of this during the interview process. As with all of these considerations, at the appropriate time you should inquire as to what their operating principles and company or team culture are.

It's important to inquire and assess the company, but you also need to use your instincts when deciding if you will be comfortable with the interviewers(s), some of which you will probably be working for and closely with.

Once you've completed your vetting checklist process, evaluate the working conditions and the sense you get from the people you came in contact with. Ask yourself: *Can I be authentic? Do the people seem happy and healthy? Do they embrace the philosophy of 'people first'?* There is nothing worse than finding out that the company you choose to work for did not embrace and live by the values you were expecting. Ask lots of questions from everyone you come in contact with during the interviewing process regarding the people side of the company's culture. When asked by the interviewers and the human resource group if you have questions, make sure that you specifically ask them to describe the culture and the value and importance they place on employee engagement. If you get a chuckle or worse, a poor response, beware, you could be walking into a volcano waiting to erupt on your life and all your efforts thus far!

If the interviewers or people you get to meet in the company aren't speaking highly about the company culture, you should pause and ask more questions.

I truly believed that my overall company and my immediate organization had a positive working culture, exuding "happy work-happy life." Because that was the case, I always made it a point to let the interviewee know this.

Here are a few of the points I would make about my specific company, as well as the group leaders they would be reporting to:

◆ Flex hours once or twice a week when necessary
◆ Alternate Fridays off to enable employees to care for personal needs
◆ Numerous required reviews per year with your manager
◆ Employee engagement surveys every year
◆ Employee engagement scores used as part of the bonus goal system
◆ Open/transparent communication
◆ Open line for confidential employee concerns
◆ Advancement and growth opportunities posted and encouraged

You could find yourself over-the-top happy, regarding all of the items on your checklist, but I can't emphasize enough, the importance you must place on how the company and your potential manager place on the value of a happy and healthy work environment. There is nothing worse than not being happy in your everyday environment.

During the last several years of my employment at Northrop Grumman, we conducted annual engagement surveys from an outside firm. Employee opinions were greatly valued. This offered a big voice to all employees and it quickly flushed out managers who were not effectively leading and caring for their teams. We all took this seriously and it didn't take long to see how this one action produced a better work environment. Happy and healthy employees usually translate into strong overall company performance.

MEDICAL BENEFITS

Medical benefits sometimes get overlooked in the decision process. In today's world, this has become extremely important for two reasons: coverage and cost. Companies may pay all of the medical cost or partial, while some may not pay at all. For a single person, this can be hundreds of dollars a month and for a family, it can go much higher. Medical coverage usually comes to light the day of orientation, so you don't want this to be a whopping negative surprise. This is a benefit that you must factor in when accessing your compensation package.

PENSION/401K PLANS

In years past, having a company pension plan was often a given, although today, it is rare that a company maintains a long-term pension plan for new employees. Since most companies don't have pension plans, it doesn't become a large deciding factor. If the company has some type of pension plan, I would view it as an additional benefit and realize that it will probably go away some time in the future.

Whether or not the company has a 401k type plan will be a glaring decision item. It may not sound important at first, but I can assure you this is a big deal. If they have a retirement investment plan, inquire about the company match (whether there is a match and what the terms are). When making your decision for employment, consider the financial benefit of company match plans.

As an example, if you were to get a $75K annual salary and you contribute 10% of your salary and the company matches 50%, you would be getting a company contribution of $3,750 per year. I look at this as "free found money" that you must take advantage of. You can also elect to contribute all or part of your personal contribution as deferred income reducing your tax exposure. Taxes will be incurred when you withdraw the money during your retirement years, which will likely be at a much lower rate as your income will be lower. Without the old-fashioned pension plans of the past, this is a must to-do. (I could write another book on this subject alone and maybe I will in the future.)

Because of its importance to your long-term financial security and independence, I am compelled to include a simple but powerful example regarding a 401K plan and the benefits of compound growth. This will hopefully spark you to think about the value of this vital financial life decision. When you understand this early in your career, you will find that *time* is your best friend when planning and maximizing your long-term retirement goals.

For purposes of furnishing you with a visual notional example, I have selected the following parameters:

Base salary	$75,000
Employee contribution 10% of salary	($7,500)
Employer contribution 5% of salary	($3,750) **(free money)**
Average rate of return	7% **(stock market historical avg.)**
Retirement age	62
Starting age	22
Timeline	40 years
Inflation adjustment	3%
Results	**Age 62**
Based on 2019 dollars	~$2,250,000

This is a very simple example that doesn't take into account your salary growth that will considerably increase the value at retirement.

(An average 3% annual raise will offset inflation rate impact.)

The values in this example will grow even larger as it grows in alignment with your income growth greater than the 3% annual average raise used in this notional example. I encourage you to search for inexpensive off-the-shelf software packages that can rapidly do endless financial forecasts. Many years ago,

I created my own software modeling tool and I utilized it all the time to help guide me towards achieving this long-term savings goal. I made a game out of it and it really became fun and exciting as I watched the values of my retirement grow over the years.

As you can see, these are large numbers, but they can only materialize if you start your 401K early. Continuously contributing some portion of your paycheck into a 401K and taking full advantage of your company's potential free contributions will be one of your most rewarding life decisions you ever make.

There is so much more I could say regarding this subject, but this *is The Brief!*

If you are planning to leave, or if for some reason, in the short term, you leave the company, there could be a "claw back clause." This means that the company may require you to be employed there for some period of time or they will eliminate all or part of the company-matched contributions. I have seen this commonly be in the range of one to three years. I don't think this should be a major factor in taking the job, but I do think it's important to know that this is their policy, so you eliminate another possible surprise in the future if you were to decide to leave.

GRADUATE SCHOOL/
<u>CONTINUING EDUCATION</u>

Depending on your future educational goals, this can be another financial consideration. Some companies do not contribute to the cost of continuing education. Companies that do contribute will have specific guidelines and maximum contributions per year that they will contribute up to. With the cost of graduate school, this can be a sizeable expense. Large companies usually have ranges of $5,000 to $20,000 per year. Once again, this can be free found money and it also needs to be part of your overall financial decision when selecting a company.

Like the 401k company-match contributions, college reimbursement plans often have a claw back feature regarding these funds. They can have windows of one to five years. If you are planning on going back to school in the near term, you should consider this before leaving the company during that window.

This can be a substantial sum of money and you don't want to be surprised downstream with this type of bill. Companies are willing to invest in their employees, but they are also going to protect their investment with some level of commitment from the employee.

PROFIT SHARING

Profit sharing is another potential compensation factor to understand and weigh during your decision process evaluation. For the purpose of placing a value on this, let's use our salary value of $75k. If a company has a profit-sharing plan with a maximum benefit of 10% of your salary, you could be looking at $7,500 of additional compensation. If the performance is not 100% achieved, the value could be based on 5%, yielding

$3,750; still a sizeable bonus or some other defined bonus/performance factor.

I would be remiss if I didn't mention that this is all based on pre-determined goals that must be achieved if employees are going to receive these bonuses. As a CFO, I was always a big supporter of incentive plans because they would motivate the work force to act more like "owners". Not to mention, sharing the wealth was a great engagement tool, again, making it a better place to work.

CAREER OPPORTUNITIES

Today's companies are more spread out over the country for various reasons and it can make it more challenging to find new opportunities unless you are open to a fair amount of relocating in the future. Make sure that there is upward mobility. If your boss doesn't have any potential growth it should tell you that this person will be what we call a "blocker". This can easily happen in a small company/department. If your plan is that you are not going to remain in this company for an extended period of time, then you could view this much differently.

COMPANY LOGISTICS

In a lot of cases, companies are located in high-cost cities where you need to see what the cost of housing and/or transportation will be. This can be another large cost that requires a cost benefit analysis. The decision of living close to work or up to sixty minutes away can be a massive financial swing. My sense is that young people today want to live close to work, but it can be pretty pricey to have this luxury. So, let's try to analyze some scenarios. What type of ex-CFO would I be if I didn't bring numbers into *The Brief*?

For example, let's evaluate the trade space between two ways of selecting where to live: The New York city area versus the outlining suburbs. These are rough notational examples for purposes of consideration.

OPTION # 1

	Per month expense	Annual
Live close to work in city environment rent cost	$2,500	$30,000
Mass transit	$125	$1,500
City tax on $75,000 salary at 6%	$375	$4,500
	$3,000	$36,000

OPTION #2

	Per month expense	Annual
Live in suburbs and rent	$1,000	$12,000
Mass transit	$400	$4,800
Car loan	$300	$3,600

Gas	$125	$1,500
Car insurance	$125	$1,500
	$1,950	$23,400

FINANCIAL ANALYSIS:

Monthly and Yearly comparisons	Per month expense	Annual
Option #1 Total housing/travel expenses	$3,000	$36,000
Option # 2 Total housing/travel expense	$1,950	$23,400
Variance	$1,050	$12,600

I only use this type of example for financial evaluation purposes, but I'm keenly aware that some young people today value their time more than money, which I can appreciate, since I always traveled fairly large distances to work. My objective here is to demonstrate another set of criteria that needs to be considered in the decision-making process.

Telecommuting is another thing that you should inquire about from your potential employer. You should especially consider this if you are leaning towards living further away from your new office. It will reduce your expenses and return some of that precious time.

As you can see by some of these key decision points, there are many things to consider beyond the obvious one, which is salary. Unfortunately, people who are excited about getting a job offer and the salary that they are given, often don't think about the other important considerations.

To summarize, let's look one more time at some of the sizeable financial concepts that should be given consideration when making your final acceptance of an offer: I've set up an example based on a $75,000 salary, a 5% company contribution added to your 401k contribution ($75,000 x 5% company contribution = $3,750), a $10,000 per year company college reimbursement and a potential maximum profit-sharing performance result of 10% of your salary:

<u>NOTIONAL ESTIMATE</u>

Salary	$75,000
401K company match	$3,750
College reimbursement	$10,000
Profit sharing	<u>$7,500</u>
Potential compensation	$96,250
Additional compensation	$21,250

When you see these values framed together, you can visualize how important these decisions can be. As I mentioned earlier, there are many financial and non-financial things that you need to evaluate so that you make a fully informed decision. Make your own personal prioritized spreadsheet and then weigh the total impact. The point here is to think through the entire offer and the value it could bring you and then *prioritize* your expectations.

CHAPTER 7

Persistence: Status Checks and Relentless Focus

"The way to get started is to quit talking and begin doing."
—WALT DISNEY

HOW OFTEN DO you create and deliver presentations? Are you skilled at PowerPoint? Do you get discouraged easily or work hard at negotiating? Are you paying full attention when others are talking? Are you confident while talking in a professional arena?

As Lee Iacocca said, "You can have brilliant ideas, but if you can't get them across, your ideas won't get you anywhere."

To work your way up the corporate ladder, it is imperative that you have developed strong communications skills. I like to describe it as the "perfect bow on the package." There are countless smart, talented, educated people in the world, but many do not have effective presentation and communication skills. My vast experience in the corporate world taught me the value of having dynamic communication skills.

Communication is fundamental in all facets of business, but it can also make the difference between obtaining the results you want or not. Having both written and verbal communication skills is critical for a leader to mature their career. It's essential to learn how to be able to effectively package/frame information. I found over time that communication was an art that needed to be mastered and to value the importance of this skill set. When coaching people in this area, I would emphasize three points as it pertained to developing presentations or other written communication forms: accuracy, clarity and brevity. Ensure that your key messages pop off the chart; don't make the audience work to understand the messages you are trying to convey. Spend the proper amount of time constructing your charts.

My method for constructing charts was to take a quick pass at building the key messages and then to begin to populate each chart with the supporting information needed to anchor the key points that I needed to get across to the audience. Whenever I went back to an audience with an updated status, I would always construct a chart up front that would simply recap our last review. From there, I would frame the key subjects and if required, updates and actions taken. This would help me stay clear on the meeting objectives and usually ward off endless questions from the start. It's essential to have control of the audience and that requires clarity, traceability and brevity.

Throughout my career, unfortunately, I've witnessed many leaders do a poor job of preparing presentations, leading to a lot of stumbling and red faces when it comes time to deliver. Once you begin to lose the confidence of senior leaders in a review, it spirals down an ugly path. I can't count the times I was complimented after given my presentations even when delivering "bad news."

It's much easier to deliver good news. However, I've seen that go bad as well because things were confusing, leaving the reviewers in a state of not truly believing the data and recommendations. I must also underscore the importance of developing potential solutions when confronted with delivering negative news. Just throwing bad news on the table without solution sets is the kiss of death!

I would intently observe senior leaders within the company and learn from their successes and failures when delivering important messages to the highest level of the company or to important customers. As I will note in the mentoring section also, being able to be the preverbeal "fly on the wall" in the "big room" where important presentations were being reviewed is invaluable.

I learned so much from being able to sit in the corporate executive reviews and witness how things are done by the best in the industry. I would observe body movement and listen to every word. I would also see how the presenter reacted when things would get loud and confrontational. Being able to defuse an audience getting out of control and getting things back into the box is another monumental skill, and it doesn't come easy. This is especially difficult when the audience is the C-suite.

You must understand how and when you can regain control in the room when multiple people are impassionately talking across each other. You go with your instincts, but it's all about timing, poise and confidence.

I would often go about this by leaving the front of the room and walk up closer to the audience in a conference room and then say something like, "Time is not my friend and I think I need to press on and take an action to further address the discussion point so actively being debated."

Then I would directly address the most senior person in the room and ask if that would be acceptable. I would be as forceful as I thought was appropriate, always keeping my composure and balancing aggressiveness with respect. This is a critical skill and often required. I learned this by observing others when I didn't have a speaking role. I've seen many colleagues get thrown off their game in this type of situation, and it's not pleasant.

In my role as a division CFO, as one would expect, a significant amount of my presentation content would involve numbers. My No. 1 rule regarding numbers was to make sure that there was continuity throughout the briefing charts and that all values tied together. There is nothing worse than executives trying to do "mental math" in the meeting, creating endless questions and confusion. No matter how good you are on your feet, you want to avoid this common occurrence. As the leader, it was my responsibility to make sure that everything was clearly thought out and vetted with my team. Since most of my presentations required data input from several organizations, it was imperative that my team and I reconstruct things where appropriate to ensure that the presentation had continuity. I would go to great lengths to make sure that everything flowed seamlessly. Quite often, presenters will just input charts from other groups without scrutinizing all of the data and making sure it doesn't contradict a prior slide or a future slide. This can be a horror.

Like most things to be successful, you must put the proper amount of time and energy into the product. When assembling my final slide package, I would perform a dry run with my core team. We would review every slide on the large screen in my office. We would access every bullet and every number.

Real-time, we would modify the slides, reorder them and take actions to bring in department heads to update data or clarify information they furnished us. The team also checked for traceability of all numbers throughout the entire presentation. I played an active role in this process because I needed to take ownership. I always over-prepared and it served me well throughout my career.

I was keenly aware that I was going to be on the stage with senior executives and it was imperative that I have my act together. As we worked the slides, I became the conductor. It was my job to listen to my team's input and to decide what changes would be made to the order of the slides and how long the presentation was going to be.

Having my team together afforded great input and constructive criticism. It also gave me the opportunity to ask questions and take side notes. Once we had the content to our liking, we would work on the "glitz" part of the presentation.

This would be where we would add simple graphs, pictures, etc. to enhance the appeal of the slides and anchor the bullet points on the chart.

It should also be mentioned that short bullet points are required and not long run-on sentences. The info should enable the presenter to start their verbal talking points. Once again, this takes practice and commitment to excellence. Not only did I spend a significant amount of time on these slides; I would also practice endlesslessy, attempting to anticipate all of the hard questions that could come to me. I learned early on to "prepare for the worst and hope for the best".

During my working sessions, I would invite key junior employees to observe and even participate. They were always taken back to just how much preparation was required when getting ready to present to the senior levels of the company and customers.

While presenting, you must be able to package and frame information effectively, whether it be good or bad news. This is truly an art and you should never underestimate its significance. Some guiding principles to be aware of and follow:

◆ Be accurate, concise, simple and clear.

◆ Ensure you are not making the audience work to understand your message.

◆ Create key takeaways to pop off your charts.

◆ Once you have the powerful chart(s), you now must be able to successfully deliver the message.

Reinforce with highlights what is visually shown on the chart and try not to read directly from the charts. The words on the chart are a guide for you to stay on message. Some level of graphics, whether it be pictures or charts as a backdrop, usually enhance the message and strengthen the appeal of the presentation, enticing the audience to stay engaged. The pizzazz of the visuals will aid in the delivery and reacceptance of the message. Without question, the content is the most important part, but a poorly laid out presentation can ruin your day.

I always did my best presenting standing and moving around the conference room. I prepared the building of my charts with my teams. I ultimately made the final decisions, but their insights were invaluable and furnished me with new ideas and perspectives. My team approach of listening to diverse opinions and thoughts was a big plus in developing my final product. Once I gained consensus from my team, I was then able to choose the most powerful approach to frame the presentation.

My key objectives whenever I was presenting to groups:

◆ Demonstrate confidence and passion.
◆ Anticipate the difficult questions.
◆ Always over-prepare.
◆ If you don't know an answer, don't fake it.
◆ Be genuine.
◆ Remain calm and remain in control.
◆ Be mindful of the clock.
◆ Be respectful no matter how challenged you get.

Throughout my career, one of my greatest strengths was my ability to rapidly build powerful messages. Don't get me wrong; this was a learning curve, but an incredibly important one for me.

I also received and graciously welcomed feedback from audiences and most importantly my senior leaders. Feedback can be tough sometimes, but ultimately building off of weaknesses and learning from mistakes is what accelerated my abilities and advancement. It was always a great compliment when other leaders would ask for my presentations so that they could format their charts in a similar manner after they saw how well they were received. In preparing for presentations, practice is essential. Like anything else, the more experience you have, the better you'll get. In my case, I practiced endlessly and it paid great dividends. Most of the time, I didn't even need to look at the chart on the screen. It enabled me to be comfortable enabling me to clearly deliver and address challenging questions.

The following are a few suggestions to help you to improve and strengthen your written and verbal communication skills:

◆ Request your manager to send you to communication training.

◆ Take a college or higher education communication or leadership class. Most of these classes will entail many presentations and commonly have a video tape component where you will be able to watch yourself present. This can be painful, but a great way to learn your strengths and weaknesses.

◆ Learn from the best; don't try to emulate any one person.

◆ If possible, ask leadership if you can shadow them when presenting to their leadership.

There's no better way to learn than to observe in a real-world setting how leaders communicate. Over the years, several of my employees asked if they could sit in on my presentations to leadership. Whenever possible, I never denied their request. Learning from watching others is one of the most effective ways to develop these skills.

I learned along the way that there are only a small number of leaders who truly have strong communication skills. Natural ability is necessary, but it is just as important to learn and hone in on your skills. This takes years of practice and plenty of mistakes!

BRIEF STORY

Titanic Training

While attending Wharton, professors underscored the value of top-notch communication skills. We spent three days with communication experts from Harvard University. Even though this was an executive class, I was quite surprised how many of us needed to strenghten our skills.

As we started out this section of the curriculum, they broke us up into groups of ten. Each person in the group had different levels of communication skills and experience. The groups would cycle through a process that would start out with a crisis topic, where we were tasked to prepare our opening remarks and then transition for Q&A.

The session was being taped and would be played back on an intimidating lecture room screen practically the size of a drive-in movie screen, for the group to review and critique.

The instructors asked if anyone wanted to volunteer to go first to get things started. Even though I was somewhat overwhelmed by the talent and positions of my classmates, I thought this would be a good place for me to jump out of my comfort zone and volunteer to go first. To this day, I don't know what I was thinking. The instructors helped guide us individually to construct the two- to three-minute opening remarks. Constructing these couple of minutes of words taught me more than I could ever explain.

Hours later, we would all reassemble back into a formal newsroom setup. As I approched the podium and microphone with two real-time TV cameras pointed at me, I rapidly began to sweat and lose my confidence. The only crutch I had were my cue cards.

The next thing I knew, the instructors were counting down 5-4-3-2-1 and "you're on." I couldn't remember what I said and it felt like forever until my time was up. What I didn't realize was that this was the easy part and what was to come next was a barrage of questions from the instructors posing as the press. I got through it and my classmates applauded. They also thanked me for going first! I was completely mortified by my poor performance.

My classmates did their parts and each one learned from the many mistakes those in front of them made. This was definitely the most stressful part of my time at Wharton, but it helped me immensely. I drew upon this experience and the knowledge I gained as I honed my communication skills going forward.

The next step was to go off with the instructor and critique the video and then work on what needed to be corrected and strenghtened. As I watched the video for the second time, I was stunned by the number of mistakes I made. I was determined to fix this. It was humbling, to say the least, as I thought I had "mastered" the art of communications.

I spent ninety minutes with the instructor, which was probably the most valuable time I have ever spent with a professor or coach. The next day, after practice and additional coaching, we went back in the mock news room to try again with another subject that we prepared for and received specific coaching on.

This time I went last. After the coaching and the luxury of watching a variety of leaders succeed and fail, I was able to make additional changes and tweaks to my approach and delivery.

On the third day, we went back to watch the videos together as a group, viewing the first and second attempt at this mock communication session. I was up first. I slumped down in my seat as we watched my performance once again on the big screen. It seemed even worse the second time I saw it. The instructors went over the good points and the things that needed work. I couldn't wait until this was over. As the instructors set up the second video, the professors thankfully stated to the group that they had "never seen such a remarkable change in skill in such a short period of coaching time." I must admit that I was really pr   oud of myself and my ability to listen, absorb and be able to make such a dramatic transformation.

The reason I share this story is because it proved to me once again how important recognizing your shortcomings is, along with receiving formal training. I was rather fortunate to have had the opportunity to have some of the best in academia coach me, even if for a couple of days.

It's hard for me to believe this happened back in 2006. Every day from that point forward, I have worked on becoming a better communicator and presenter.

I had a one-on-one session with the communications professor, which lasted about ninety minutes. During that relatively short period of time, she went through all of the things that I did wrong and the things I did right, which was a significantly smaller list.

She knew that I was embarrassed and perplexed, since I had a lot of confidence in my communication skills. She told me that I had all the qualities of a strong communicator. She also conveyed to me that if I followed her guidance I would make a real change in performance. She told me that I was understandably nervous. Having TV cameras right up close and my coworkers watching my every move was, to say the least, intimidating. She also appreciated me going first, but that made it even harder because I did not have the ability to observe others before me. She thought I was moving my body around too much behind the podium and my hands were also moving too much. She attributed a lot of this to the fact that I usually present with a microphone attached to me, allowing me to move freely around the stage or room. She quickly made me understand that standing behind the podium is an entirely different messaging approach. She expressed that I had natural talent in this area.

In addition to my excessive movement during my mock presentation to the press, she thought I was trying too hard during the Q&A session, trying to answer each question with a laborious answer. The professor underscored the importance of not giving too much information, as it can and usually does open you up too many more questions. She said the same thing could happen in a corporate review environment as well.

She recommended taking a short pause to think about my answer and to keep the answer clear and short. Often, people believe that if they give a long answer, they will impress the audience. What happens is that you usually go off message and trip yourself up, commonly bringing new unnecessary information into the discussion.

At the end of our session, she reassured me that I had strong communication skills and that I have the likeability factor going for me.

She encouraged me to relax, incorporate her suggestions and remain confident. She also emphasized the importance of always staying in control.

The professor's advice was spot on and I realized just how good she was at teaching these skills.

COMMUNICATIONS BRIEF

◆ Be prepared.

◆ Stay calm and keep your composure.

◆ Don't read your messages unless there is a specific required statement where every word is critical to the situation.

◆ Move your eyes around the room; make good eye contact with all members in the room.

◆ When standing behind the podium, don't move around too much.

◆ Try not to ad-lib too much.

◆ Don't stray off message.

◆ Don't say more than you need to (less is sometimes more).

◆ Understand your audience.

◆ When answering questions, don't stray off topic.

◆ Be conscience of your body language as it sends its own type of messages.

◆ If you don't have an answer to a question, let them know that you will follow up; don't wing it with a bad inaccurate answer.

◆ Stay upbeat; likeability helps even when delivering difficult news.

◆ Remain in control of the audience.

The ability to effectively communicate when dealing with customer negotiations is another area where these skills can pay great dividends. Your delivery, poise, body language, data preparation, confidence, etc. all play a vital role if you are going to influence a positive outcome.

Even when the opposing team has what may seem as the upper-hand you can shift the momentum with the ability to convey key points and arguments, influencing a potentially different outcome. I've watched others and I personally accomplished this more times than I can count in my career.

It's a lot easier to come out a winner in a negotiation or in a management review when you have the facts and supporting backup to defend your case. Although I've seen some very smart, well-prepared people lose their case because they had a poorly laid out presentation and an even worse delivery. My communication skills, coupled with my preparation, enabled me to get through many tough senior reviews where others sometimes got destroyed.

A technique I would also utilize in senior management reviews was to move around instead of speaking from a podium. A lot of other presenters would not abandon the podium since that's where their prepared notes were. Leaving that space would separate them from potentially needed "life lines." I prided myself on knowing my data and a great memory that I didn't need my backup charts. Don't get me wrong—I had more notes on my hard copy slides almost to the point where you couldn't read them. It was my way of practicing and as I previously mentioned, I worked closely with my team experts when creating my presentations and key takeaways. Admittedly, I practiced to the point of crazy sometimes! My motto was "prepare for the worst and hope for the best."

I would guess that 75% of people feel comfortable behind a podium, whereas I felt most comfortable being able to drift around the room. This takes skill as well because you don't want to move around so much that it's distracting to the audience and can make you look nervous and unprepared. I would usually stand in one place and shift from one side of the room to the other to keep their attention on me and my message. When I thought it was required, I would move closer to key leaders or participants in the room to show them that I valued their input.

I would make sure that I approached them slowly demonstrating respect and confidence.

I was often presenting to the corporate CEO, CFO, COO, government and senior military leaders, so I needed to be meticulous in my delivery. Fortunately, I had good instincts and the ability to control the room even when it was filled with executives. Note that there will be times when a strong personality in the meeting will try to show how smart they are and will get confrontational with you. In these cases, don't get physically closer to the individual because that could further ignite them and totally derail a good outcome for *your* presentation. This takes time to learn. Attempt to practice many times at lower levels in the organzation long before you go on the big stage.

One evening, I was at a speaking engagement at the University of Florida where I often spoke. Of course, I was spending a lot of time on the backend of the talk discussing the importance of strong communication skills.

After one of these sessions, a group of students went to get the department head of communications office. They were quite energized and impressed with the amount of time I spent on the subject of communication. During the tail end of my talk, a couple of the students went directly to their communications department head professor. They quickly conveyed to the professor what I was saying about the importance of strong communications. About ten minutes later, they returned with the professor.

He said he had to come to meet me, as his students were genuinely excited and quite impressed with what I was saying to them. What really got the professor excited was when the students told him that I said "good communication skills is like having the perfect bow on top of the present." The professor thanked me for highlighting the significance. He made the point that professors can teach the students things that they will need to know, but it really resonates when a corporate America executive reinforces its importance.

THOSE MOMENTS WITH MANAGEMENT

Learning how to effectively work with your boss is mutually paramount. At every level this becomes a critical ingredient regarding your success in meeting your boss's objectives. Sometimes you get a boss (leader) who makes this easy on the employee, but you may get a boss who is not people-oriented and doesn't value the importance of a happy and healthy employee. It was my trademark to ensure that my organizations had high employee engagement scores, always felt that their voice counted and that they were a valuable part to the success of the company.

Throughout my career, I was told that I had a unique talent for being a caring and nurturing leader, which isn't the norm in a challenging, high-stress business environment. Bottom line results are usually superior. And many bosses will press hard and not take the time to explain the mission or give clear enough direction. Many bosses expect employees to "just figure it out" and lack approachability. This often causes great anxiety for the employee and they become frozen and ineffective.

Unfortunately, some bosses manage by fear or just a lack of understanding how important it is to spend quality time with your employees. I can't tell you how many times I've heard from employees or people I mentor how much they dislike their boss and have little to no respect for them.

I'm not suggesting that you need to be able to run to your boss with every problem, but I do recommend that you do go to them when you are confused or having difficulty performing your given assignment.

I believe my teams were always successful and respected because I fostered a culture where employees felt safe and valued and knew that they could always come to me or their immediate manager if they needed help and support. I also want to make sure that I'm totally candid and let you know that there were moments that I did not live up to this when under enormous pressure to get something to my superiors.

I would, however, explain to my team that things were going to be crazy and out of norm on those rare occasions. I would also follow up with them after the crisis was over and thank them for their patience and understanding. I would try to give it my best effort during these highly stressful times to pause, especially when a director or manager would inform me that the team was struggling.

At that point, I would reflect on how I would want to be treated by my boss during these times and I would give my total dedication for a boss that was inconsiderate and unapproachable. During those moments, I knew it was my job to lead the team and to be their cheerleader, not just another uncaring boss.

When I took the time to explain critical objectives and timelines that I was given from my superiors, the team could then have a greater appreciation for my urgency. I would take the time to clearly frame the objectives and goals, work through the method and path to best get us to the finish line, minimizing stress and the unknown. This also gave me the ability to see if I was being realistic and if appropriate, change course.

For the early career professionals, it can be quite daunting when the boss gives little direction when assigning an important quick turnaround task. If you are not working for a hands-on compassionate leader, I recommend you try to set up some time with them to further discuss the assignment. I know that confronting your boss can be a little scary, but it almost always turns out with a fairly good result if *you* handle it correctly.

I recommend you first telling the boss that you understand the urgency of the assignment and that you are there to make sure that you meet the expectations by knowing exactly what is needed.

Realize that the boss is most likely under significant pressure and not thinking about anything other than "I need my stuff." You can actually help them here by asking them to spend a little of their valuable time framing the assignment, giving it additional clarity.

More times than not, when they pause and take a breath to describe the information needed, they will either discover that they don't really know what they need or better yet, they will give the insight and direction you need to have a better chance of finishing the task with the best product possible within the allotted timeframe.

The light bulb will go on for both you and your boss. This will also give you both the ability to quickly collaborate and come up with a solid plan to follow. You could also let the boss know that you will come by with an interim look at your progress, ensuring that things are progressing. There is nothing worse than finding out at the end of the timeframe that things are not going to meet the expectations. You will sometimes meet resistance, but I recommend that you be *persistent* as this will most often save you and your boss from failure, which is what you want to avoid.

Every boss is different and some may not support this approach of being more engaged with their workforce, but the majority, if given the chance, will give you the time you request. If that happens, go prepared with specific questions and ideas that you can bounce off of them.

Your goal for the meeting should be two-fold: first, get clarity, and then demonstrate your ability to think creatively and strategically offering up ways to better approach the project. When you get that time with your boss, make them aware of any current or potential roadblocks that could slow down or derail the process. If you are not getting the support from other organizations, you may need their help to intercede.

These short sessions will probably clear up a lot of things and also demonstrate to the boss how serious and dedicated you are to achieving and exceeding their expectations.

CAUTION: Don't use this valuable time to whine and complain. Stay positive and deliberate on getting what you need. After this session, you will be less stressed, which will better enable you to think and perform with more clarity and confidence. One thing I can guarantee you is that you will deliver a much better product after that meeting. Driving with your eyes closed and being afraid to open them will be disastrous.

Asking practical questions will open up the dialogue and it will serve you well in the end game. You will sometimes meet resistance, but you must be persistent and somewhat courageous. It sounds scary, but it truly isn't. This extra time will likely save you and your boss from a possible disaster.

If you find yourself working for a boss who is not receptive to your questions, concerns and overall wellbeing, it's probably time to think about exploring new opportunities. There is nothing worse than working for an arrogant, non-caring boss. Do not let it cause you great anxiety, as it's not worth it. Going to a job every day that you dislike is not healthy.

If it comes to looking for a new job, make sure you are even more inquisitive regarding your potential new boss's leadership style and the culture of their group.

NEXT STEPS ON YOUR LADDER—PROMOTIONS

It can intimidating and stressful when thinking about going to your boss to discuss you career trajectory and even harder to bring up the word "raise." I give this advice to my mentees and my own grown professional children. My general guidance is to set up a meeting with your boss; don't try to accomplish this with a drive-by of her office. This shouldn't be a surprise attack, but rather, needs to be a professional meeting. When setting up the meeting, name the subject something similar to: "Personal performance check-in" or something along those lines.

When you get the meeting on the calendar, prepare your messaging and be mindful of the time they have allotted for you. Go into this meeting prepared, and try to keep it simple, nonconfrontational, upbeat and succinct. Make sure you come out of the meeting with an outcome. If you are highly frustrated with your status and compensation and you are preparing or already searching for new opportunities, make sure that you are making the right move at the right time. More times than not, the boss just hasn't given it the proper time to think about the value you bring to the organization and it often requires a delicate but strong wake-up call.

Succinctly rattle off your most recent accomplishments and your consistent high level of performance. Reinforce the point that you are committed to excellence, and you have proven to be a consistently high performer. Try to start off the conversation with many positives, setting the stage for you to introduce your concerns, as they relate to your position and career growth.

I would then begin to calmly voice your concerns. Let her know that you don't feel valued and are frustrated and concerned that there isn't enough upward mobility or monetary rewards for you. I wouldn't make it any more complicated than that. It takes a little courage, but you will feel much better after you get these frustrations off your mind.

Unfortunately, most people don't have this meeting and remain frustrated and unhappy in their job. A short discussion will make the manager recognize both that they could be losing you and the grief and disruption this would eventually cause them and the overall success of the team and enterprise.

If you haven't heard back from your boss regarding your accomplishments and concerns in several weeks, go back to them with a refresh of your last conversation. You planted the "seed" in their mind on your first meeting; now you must "water the seed" to ensure that it will grow, sprouting the "fruit" it needs to manifest.

My managers and I have sometimes received this type of subtle message from a key employee, making us realize that we needed to evaluate just how important this individual was to us and the enterprise. Even though my team and I were engaged with our employees, there were times that we missed the mark. I've seen other organizations and companies that were not properly caring for their high performers really experience a wake-up call.

I can't tell you how many times I've seen people not go to their boss to address their concerns. Eventually the employee gets another offer from a company, informs his/her boss and the boss rapidly comes back with a counter offer. At that point, it's usually too late. This probably could have all been avoided if the employee had spoken up. I recommend this approach for an employee who's happy with the company and the people, but for some reason, they aren't being properly motivated and taken care of.

If you do meet with your boss and they don't get the hint, it will at least make things a lot easier on you when you inform them that you're leaving. This happens way too often and it shouldn't.

CHAPTER 8

Patience: Climbing, Stumbling, Leaping

"Adopt the pace of nature; her secret is patience."
—RALPH WALDO EMERSON

DO YOU KNOW how to sink into the moment? Do you think that anything worth putting your effort toward is worth waiting for? When was the last time that you waited a long time for something worthwhile without rushing it? Has someone in business called you impatient?

Again, working your way up the corporate ladder is a journey and not a sprint. This is a valuable lesson to learn right out of the gate. We all want to make more money and get promoted rapidly. When speaking to early career employees, I would underscore the importance of being patient. I would give them the tough love talk, while letting them know how much I wanted to help them grow and succeed. Most of the time, I was successful in gaining the respect and confidence of these young and impressionable talented people. I often found that they really didn't know how the real world worked and once they believed in me they opened up, wanting to know what it would take to succeed and what the best plan of action would be. One of the greatest best rewards of my career as a leader was seeing how I could gain the confidence of these smart and energetic young talents.

I would take the time to understand their goals and aspirations. Once they were comfortable with me, they would open up and want to learn, asking endless questions.

I truly enjoyed imparting my knowledge and experience to the generation of the future. To me there was nothing more rewarding than helping young people and being part of their professional growth journey.

I would reinforce with new hires recently out of college how things worked inside companies and how they should set their expectations. Most engineering and manufacturing high-tech companies are structured this way.

Banks and finance-related companies have a much different hierarchy system. In a company like Northrop Grumman within the business management organization there was a career ladder:

◆ Entry levels 1-5
◆ First / Second (Line Manager)
◆ Department Manager
◆ Business Manager
◆ Director, Business Management

- Division Vice President CFO (11 steps to the position I retired from)
- Sector Vice President
- Corporate VP and CFO

Once I laid out all the levels, I would then break down each job description for them and the type of experience and education required to attain them. I would also explain the technical and leaderships skills needed to attain each position. As I've mentioned several times, the career growth plan is a journey and it gets more demanding with every step. To emphasize the point, I would give some perspective with hard data as follows.

Below are the percentages of people in the company that achieve the middle to senior-level management positions where the challenges and the financial rewards can be significant and life-changing.

Out of a population of 85,000 employees, which is a large corporation, the percent of employees that are able and willing to attain leadership positions are as follows (approximate figures for a high-tech company similar to Northrop Grumman):

- Manager 20%
- Directors 3%
- Vice Presidents .2%

I would tell each one of my employees that they are capable of great things, but they must have their eyes wide open to how many people actually attain middle to senior-level positions and what the requirements and sacrifices are that come with these positions. This requires skill, education, leadership skills, commitment, personal investment, sacrifice and a little bit of luck and timing.

This real-world discussion supported by real data makes them all pause. Once I have them understanding, we then transition to the next step of how and what it takes to make these career steps. Now, it gets interesting and fun and at the same time we are keeping it real.

I also frame a couple of other key points that are to be expected inside a major corporation:

◆ High expectations
◆ Fast-paced environment
◆ Goal oriented
◆ Highly competitive
◆ Continuous management changes
◆ Politics
◆ Ability to adapt to changing requirements

My goal was to give these young, exuberant employees a real picture while keeping them highly motivated and excited about their current positions and the opportunities that lie ahead for them.

Once the early career employees understand the growth path and that ~20% of employees achieve mid-level management and ~3% achieve the most senior levels of the company's leadership team, they are ready to grasp what it really takes to reach the management levels.

These discussions would then begin to shift to what it takes to chart your course and what the associated rewards and sacrifices are. I carefully explain to them that it's their career and they need to invest in themselves—that requires time and commitment. That requires *patience*!

These are a few of the recommendations I often give them as they prepare to chart their course of action. My advice is to take small bites as they try to consume the preverbal elephant:

◆ Continuous education graduate school
◆ Internal/external training
◆ Search out rotation programs
◆ Develop strong communication skills
◆ Demonstrate high energy
◆ Be dependable
◆ Work hard every day

RESULTS

◆ More responsibility
◆ Greater challenges

- Lead versus follow
- Personal satisfaction
- Personal commitment
- Increased stress
- Higher salary
- Incentive compensation (bonus, stock awards, special awards)

When developing your short-term career plan, stay realistic and you should share it with your mentor(s) before reviewing it with your immediate manager. Set expectations for yourself and share them with your manager. Solicit their feedback and expectations of you. Communicate your learning desires and how you can continue to strengthen your skills in parallel to doing a great job in your current position. Always make sure that your learning aperture is wide open.

Stretch yourself within reason and find ways to diversify your skills. With today's technology tools, you can learn just about everything. Seek out subject matter experts in the organization and ask them lots of questions. These experts are almost always willing to share their expertise. Your day job comes first, but if you use your time wisely you can learn lots of other skills in parallel. Exercise patience. Learning is cumulative. It takes time to learn something new and apply it.

Once you have spent an appropriate time in your current position, don't allow yourself to get complacent and fall into the trap of being comfortable. Also, beware of some managers who will inadvertently stifle your learning and growth progress because they don't want to lose you. I observed many leaders who did not support their key employees' career growth because of the immediate impact to their departments. When I saw this type of behavior, I would immediately meet with the manager and explain the importance of helping the star employee grow—it was part of their leadership responsibility.

I would also reinforce the importance of them building a strong benchmark for the overall group to be stronger, as well as making it a lot smoother transition when the key employee moved to another opportunity.

When people see and hear that organizations are supportive of career growth and that they believe it helps the health of the company, they want to be part of that type of team. Most managers that I spoke to about this would get it, but sometimes I would confront a manager who just wouldn't get on board to that type of leadership culture. Sometimes I had to make a tough decision to remove that manager from their current role because they were not believers.

There is a big difference between someone that manages and someone that leads. Cultivate talent: This is the culture that I instilled in my organization and it always paid great dividends to the overall success my enterprise.

It's imperative that everyone have several coaches of diverse backgrounds and if possible, a senior-level manager or executive. Recognize that there is a difference between a coach and a mentor. Seeking one out who is suitable for you takes time.

EMPOWERMENT AND ENCOURAGEMENT—THE COACH

A coach is someone who gives their perspective and shares advise according to their own experiences. When selecting coaches, look for people who have proven to be successful. Receiving multiple opinions and paths enable you to see things through different and unique lenses assisting you to think with an open mind. They can help in guiding you in the right direction. Most will be able to open doors for you and introduce you to a new network of contacts.

CONFIDANTE AND LIFETIME ENHANCEMENTS—THE MENTOR

Do you have a mentor? I can't tell you how many times I have received the answer, *no*, from some very educated, smart people.

A mentor is someone you trust sharing personal information with. The mentor should be a person who has a strong reputation with the highest level of integrity. This successful leader will have influence in the organization, which will enable you to gain advocacy across and up the slippery corporate ladder. This mentor will be able to share the good, the bad and the ugly within the ranks of the organization. This will help guide you through the very dynamic and usually political environment.

They will also be able to give you the formula for strengthening your capabilities and for what it takes to work your way up the organizational ranks. They can give you explicit examples of what happens behind the large corporate doors of leadership. The biggest thing you must remember when working with a senior leader is to keep all of your discussions private unless the mentor gives you the green light to share with others.

It's imperative that there be total trust between both the mentee and the mentor. When selecting your mentor(s), look for someone that you admire and respect. Find someone who will be open and honest with you. This person should also be a motivator and pusher. Once you and the mentor agree to work together, plan to meet on a regular basis.

Mentoring is voluntary, temporary, career/business/life supportive, oriented towards personal growth and mutually beneficial.

I personally *coached* countless employees who requested my time and expertise. I never said no to a request, which drove my administrator crazy, as she had the difficult task of finding me the time to meet with these individuals. She knew how much I enjoyed helping and passing on my knowledge, so she always found a way for me to spend varying degrees of time with the ones that were really serious in seeking out my help and guidance. On the other hand, I only *mentored* a handful of people. These were individuals where I was making a substantial commitment and would require me to make sure that my calender would be able to allot the appropriate time to these important commitments. Because it was so important to me, I would spend time during lunch, after hours or even weekends with these mentees.

It would be an understatement to say I had a busy schedule, but I knew that I had to have formal weekly scheduled meetings with my mentees, giving it a high priority. These sessions would ussually last an hour. Quite often, my executive assistant would need to professionally interrupt my sessions as they often ran over the scheduled time.

I loved mentoring so it was always a rewarding part of my week. I recommend having structure to these sessions, as well as establishing goals and objectives.

Of course, I always let my mentees know that I would do my best to modify my availability if they needed to speak to me before our next scheduled meeting.

This would periodically happen and I always found the time to speak with them. My executive assistant knew how important my commitment to these mentees was, and she did a great job getting them quick access to me. When starting out with a new mentee, I would discuss the importance of structure and formality, but I was also clear that informal chats were welcomed and encouraged.

When meeting for the first time in a formal setting, I would ask my mentees the types of things they needed my help with. This question usually baffles the mentee! The first thing I would then do was lighten things up and try to put them at ease. From there, we would work our way through the next steps. At this point, I would usually get out a piece of paper and sketch out thoughts regarding the path forward.

We would discuss current job pros and cons, status within their organization, frustrations, observations, potential road blocks and top-level, near-term goals and objectives. Once we got going, the discussions would become more fluid and things would start to get more relaxed. My No. 1 goal would be to establish an environment that would enable them to feel comfortable and to ensure them that I was there to help and not judge or command the sessions.

I would also do my best to make it a light-hearted session. I'm happy to be able to say that it always worked and the conversation would begin to flow better and real progress would take place.

We would also chat about family, outside work interests, and so on. We would develop an important mentor/mentee relationship where the trust and confidentiality began to take shape. I use the word "trust," but I would be remiss if I didn't underscore the point that trust is earned and it doesn't happen overnight.

After several sessions of getting to know each other, I would begin to pivot and steer the discussions towards a more formal meeting, never getting too serious but recognizing the need to put a structure together. I would ask my mentee to identify their top three near-term goals, along with a reasonable timeline to measure progress. Almost every time, the mentee would come back to me saying how difficult this request was.

This wasn't because it was technically challenging; it was the difficulty of being able to really nail down their goals and objectives and reduce it to writing. Knowing this, I always let them struggle through it with me. This process opened their eyes to the fact that they needed a plan from which to measure progress—even through usual busy days and getting increasingly consumed with their current daily assignments and challenges.

I would also emphasize that you can work really hard and do a great job, but you can easily find yourself running in place and not making much forward progress. Why? No plan!

As we progressed, I would help them sketch out a plan usually spanning over an eighteen-month period. I would work closely with them to carefully identify three skills that we would agree would streghten their ability to move to the next level. Once we agreed on these skills, we would document them on a formal timeline schedule.

From here, I would help them with the "how" part of these objectives. To facilitate things, I would direct them to subject matter experts in the company and/or specific training courses. If I thought it was required, I would also advocate for their direct line management to assign them to an outside university course. In most cases, communication training was one of the three skills that we would focus on. It was also exciting for me when I saw how enthusiastic they became once they saw this planning process begin to solidify into something concrete.

They could now see an actual plan instead of just talking about it. Don't get me wrong—the open chatting sessions were always quite valuable, but they needed to be anchored by this formal, measurable goal planning. In addition, I would invite my mentees to shadow me at key meetings and working sessions. This gave them the opportunity to see how and what happens during senior-level meetings.

Serving as a CFO of a major business within a fortune 150 company gave me visibility that effected almost every facet of the business. With this in mind, I thought it was important for mentees to shadow some of my key meetings with coworkers and other senior executives. Again, I would emphasize the importance of confidentiality.

During our regular sessions, we would discuss what took place in the meeting. I would then be able to give them thoughts involving numerous subjects. This offered the mentees insight into what gets discussed at the executive level and how valuable data is to the decision-making process. It also gave them a front row viewing seat, enabling them to observe the many different styles of executives. This was invaluable experience.

Another important point I would discuss with my mentees was the value of having leadership advocacy across the enterprise. As I mentioned in the networking section, I made it a priority to get my mentees to meet with other senior leaders in multiple areas of the company. What I tried to make clear was that hard work, strong overall skills, optomistic personality, etc are critical ingredients needed if someone is going to be able to work their way up the company and receive a commensurate compensation package. The more difficult point to get across to them is the significant benefits of having extensive advocacy across the company at both the middle and senior levels. Advocay can indeed, tilt the scales for an individual's career trajectory. Very often, we would have numerous execctives in a room for many hours to discuss and evaluate individuals that had been identified by their management for succession planning, promotions, merit increase, bonuses and stock awards. I have watched and influenced many of these decisions, yielding both positive and negative results. Within these high-level executive employee career reviews, advocacy and name recognition usually make an enormous difference in the final outcomes. It goes without saying that you must have the skills and accomplishments, but that is not a guarantee that things will always work out accordingly.

Explore ways to meet people in the company at all levels and always be on your "A" game. Leaders are always observing and developing opinions, so be aware that you are being evaluated. Project yourself with a positive attitude. Having and displaying an upbeat personality catches leaders' attention. Be known as the person who gets things done and can be counted on. If your mentor(s) or coach(s) are in the room, your chances of receiving the proper recognition is significantly boosted.

ONCE UPON A TIME IN A NEW POSITION

Now that you are inside the company, tap into the company's internal systems. Find as many organizational charts as you can. Make copies and place them in a folder for quick reference. Familiarize yourself with your direct management chain, along with organizations across the company. It helps to match pictures and names of the senior leadership. You never know when you could come in contact with a company leader. Keep your eyes and ears open at all times. Be very cognizant of your surroundings. In general, you should become painstakingly familiar with the company's websites.

Once you have achieved your goal of securing a position within a company, it's then time to transition into the mode of learning and growing. I like to start off with simple but very valuable advice for employees during their first ninety days up to first year in their new position:

◆ Make a positive first impression.
◆ Meet lots of people.
◆ Be proactive.
◆ Demonstrate strong resourcefulness.
◆ Stay focused.
◆ Work hard.
◆ Network.
◆ Have high but balanced energy.
◆ Be dependable.

My advice is to search out and associate yourself with the "winners/doers" in the office. Unfortunately, the people who most often seek you out are the ones that have too much time on their hands and are the low performers. The achievers are often too busy and consumed with their work to seek you out. Using your instincts, reach out to those hardworking employees and see how you may be able to help them.

Observe what is going on in your new business environment. Make friends with your colleagues that you can see are doing most of the heavy lifting. Likeability, hard work, resourcefulness and a positive, proactive demeanor will be noticed.

In all of my management roles in corporate America, I can tell you that my team and I could always tell from the first couple of days and the following weeks and months if we made a good hire. The qualities and personality of certain individuals would stand out and there would usually be a consensus about the recent hire.

Even when I was at the vice president level, I would receive feedback about impressive new hires.

During my visits to our numerous sites, I would ask my management team to introduce me to their recent hires and I could usually see why my management team felt so positive about certain individuals. The point I'm trying to emphasize here is that establishing early, consistent, strong impressions makes a big difference in the way you are perceived throughout the organization.

Hard work pays off, but it surely isn't a given. Be conscientious, creative, resourceful, team oriented, a strong communicator, driven, knowledgeable, a continuous learner and politically astute. Most of all, love what you do and have a strong sense of purpose as it relates to the enterprise. Show that you care about the people around you. There is no one simple answer to tell you how to succeed. Thus, the 6 P's!

You simply can't focus every day on when you will get promoted to the next step; rather, you need to stay focused on your performance, as well as your team, and leadership will recognize your value. I saw many potential leaders fail to grow because they were more worried about their personal status and disregarded the overall wellbeing of the company and the people.

Always work hard and with purpose and gain advocacy across the enterprise. Each day will build on the next. Be mindful to the fact that nothing happens overnight.

Political astuteness is essential in the real world of corporate America. Many view this as being pretentious or phony. I would reinforce the point to my key employees that being respected and sought after is important to the rise of your career. Be aware of who the leaders are that are making the big decisions regarding career growth and compensation.

There is office politics among managers and at the senior levels of the company, and they all have some degree of influence on the trajectory of your career. Understand how important it is to be respected and valued. Do not take it for granted that it will "take care of itself." Name and accomplishment recognition will be required.

I will now give you some real-world insight into how some of these career and compensation decisions are really made. First, I will start with the traditional promotion process within your organization. Most of the time, your immediate manager will be putting you in for a promotion and commensurate salary increase and that's why it's so important that the manager value you and respect you as a person, leader and technical talent. Very often, these promotions go to the director level for approval and may even go up to a vice president.

I bring this up to underscore the importance of having advocacy as far up the chain of command as possible. It becomes so much easier when all levels of the management team know you or have consistently heard good things about you. How will you summarize your personal investment? Every day counts, and outstanding performers always have a way of standing out of the crowd. Integrity, poise, presence and confidence will also define you as your career is being weighed by leadership.

Here is some inside scope, as it pertains to the yearly performance evaluation and ranking process. Sometime around the end of each year, directors and vice presidents would get together and spend one to two days reviewing employee ratings, bonuses and stock awards.

Entering into this process every year amazed me how we as a group of leaders were able to get consensus regarding these important compensation decisions. There was always lively debate regarding each leader's opinion and recommendations.

At times, it would get heated in the room and sometimes uncomfortable when we got down to the last 25 percent of key employees that would be positioned in the top two rankings, which was usually 20 percent of the total organizational population. This was sizeable money for employees and there was always more strong candidates worthy of a high ranking and additional compensation than there were slots.

During these two days, we made extremely difficult decisions and at times, it got tense. Most of the time, our decisions as a voting group were very good, but there were times that it got to be a little of a popularity contest. I think we had a really strong process in the final analysis.

The biggest reason for me including this process with you is to once again sensitize you to the real-world facts that advocacy in the workplace can influence important outcomes. When we were debating the value and the ability of key individuals and their commensurate financial rewards, it would be vital for a leader in the room to go to bat for an individual performer. That leader needed to also have done a good job outside the room over the course of time advocating for the individual with other leaders.

Once the debating starts and the voting begins, it's all about being a known commodity. I can tell you that I would lobby for key people throughout the year and when we got in the conference room for those two days, my job was to come out successfully with the votes required to support the people that I believed were worthy. Some leaders did this better than others.

In this conference room setting, we used a technique where we had an HR professional control a computer file that all of the vice presidents had inputted data into. The files were fully integrated and summarized by the employee ratings.

The rating system went as follows:

◆   5.... Superior
◆   4.... Excellent
◆   3.... Good
◆   2.... Fair
◆   1.... Poor

There were parameters and ranges by rating level, guiding us regarding the percent of merit increase available. We would always go over the number of 4 and 5 (highest) ratings. We would rapidly examine hundreds of employees, viewing the files on a large screen. On the fly, we would review each employee rating. For many employees, we would agree on the rating during the first pass. With others, we would have a spirited debate before we came to a consensus decision. Once we reached our maximum number of 5 ratings we would then take those names and put them on the top of the 4-rating list. We would then repeat the process and move the bottom 4-rating names to the 3-rating list.

This rating evaluation process determines the size of an employee's raise, and eligibility for promotions, bonuses and stock awards.

Whenever I gave this insight to my mentees and others, they were usually taken back as to how things really got determined. I would always stress the importance of knowing that the top spots were limited to the top 20% and the competition is intense. I also shared with them the big stuff that our leadership review team would consider when making these decisions. Again, advocacy and a strong reputation is vitally important.

You must impress your direct leadership, but it is also very important to be recognized by other leaders in the company. Leaders rapidly formulate assessments of employees and those thoughts can really take hold, good or bad. It's easy to lose a high rating and a lot more difficult to impress and break into the 4/5 rating club.

I can remember those times when I went to the wall for an employee that I thought was deserving of a higher rating and other leaders did not agree with me. It would sometimes require the senior vice president to make the final decision. This only happened a few times, where we just could not come to a consensus or a leader would not give in. My leaders almost always backed me up; I would attribute that to them having full confidence in my judgement, since I had a strong track record of identifying and coaching high-potential employees. The bottom line was that I had enough clout to push and secure my way. There were those rare occasions where I couldn't get my way, but I would at least set the stage for the next negotiation.

You must realize that you can work hard and be a strong performer and still find yourself not making the cut. Remain determined and learn how to play the political game. This can be a delicate process at times, but it is often required to help propel you through the tough, competitive process. That's why it is so important to have numerous coaches and influential mentors who are willing to go to bat for you and support your immediate boss.

At the appropriate time, discuss the rating and compensation process that your company utilizes with your boss. Things are carried out differently in every company, but having strong advocacy always helps your cause. Once again, this takes determination and hard work. Be persistent and patient and good things will eventually happen. Remember "the cream always rises to the top".

The succession planning process was conducted in a similar manner. Over time, the people who climb up the corporate ranks are those that leaders believe bring value to their organizations and the overall corporation. Every day builds upon itself. Those employees who understood the process would search out leaders like myself to solicit support and ask for guidance. Most leaders really want to help and most employees are either too intimidated or they just don't want to take the time and effort to reach out. Don't allow yourself to be one of these employees.

My advice here is to stay connected to your leader and mentors all year long; don't just pop up on their radar screen prior to year-end evaluations. As you can see, nothing comes easy, so you must be focused on the prize every day by impressing as many leaders as possible with your abilities, dedication and character. Once you understand the game, the rest is just up to you. Strive to be the best at what you do and it will serve you well.

I continue to support and watch the progress of many of my mentees and it is extremely rewarding to see them getting promoted into key leadership roles. It gets to a point where a leader can almost predict with a high degree of certainty, which employees will rise through the organization.

CHAPTER 9

Lifetime of Learning...
for Steady Growth

"I measure my own success as a leader by how well the
people who work for me succeed."

—MARIA SHI

ONCE YOU GRADUATE from college and join the workforce,
you will need to be mindful that you will need to continue to
get some type of informal or formal training on a regular basis. I
would recommend speaking to your manager and looking into
possible training courses that they could send you to. I would
also think hard about going to graduate school and weigh the
benefits to your overall growth plan.

Throughout my career, I would see the busiest, most dedicated people looking for more training. Continuous learning
keeps your mind fresh and blossoms with different ways at
looking at things.

As I mentioned, I went back for my MBA while leading a
department in my company and having two small children at
home. It wasn't easy, although it was exciting and challenging.

Without a doubt, getting my MBA taught me a lot about things that I needed to know while attempting to climb the corporate ladder. It also gave me the opportunity to meet other students who were working in other industries, giving me exposure to diversity of thought. My timing was good because I was gaining new knowledge involving accounting, finance, management, etc., that I could apply to my current business position.

One example was when I was in a graduate finance class and we were learning and running cash flow analyses and evaluating the financial positions of multiple companies in similar industries. Because I was doing this type of finance evaluations at work, it really reinforced the real-world value of the class and made me more inquisitive in the classroom. I found myself engulfed in learning and asking questions of my professors and classmates.

I'm a giant proponent of going to graduate school once you are in the workforce, and have time to decide what you really have a passion for, and what type of degree will strengthen you and your growth path and passion. I know there is a valuable argument that's it's a lot easier to get your degree right after undergrad and before you start in the workforce. There is no doubt that's it's an easier path, but I've seen so many people go in different directions once they start working. As I mentioned, it's really eye-opening and much more valued when you can see it applied in the job that you're in or the job that you are reaching to attain. I should also mention that my company paid for it, which many do. Either way, it's an important valuable tool.

In addition to getting my MBA, I was extremely fortunate that my company went to great expense to send me to executive training at The Wharton School. This was a game changer for me and again, I was lucky because the timing was right because a VP CFO position was going to open up in the imminent future; these positions are fairly rare. The time I spent at Wharton was incredibly valuable, as it opened my eyes up to new and different ways to think more strategically and more globally. It really positioned me well for the opportunity that presented itself one year later. As I always say, hard work, sacrifice, and natural ability are needed to grow to the executive level, but never forget that a little luck and timing go a long way. My point is that you always want to be the best prepared because you never know when you will collide with an opportunity that you never saw coming. In addition to these big events, I always searched for training classes inside of the company.

Looking back, I should share that there wasn't one role that I took on in the company where I didn't initially think I was over my head. With encouragement, I always took on the challenge, but I can assure you I was usually nervous about what I was walking into. Fortunately, with hard work, tenacity and good teammates, I always ended up doing well. Take some chances with your career and stretch yourself. It's sometimes uncomfortable, but it usually works out well and you are continuously growing and positioning yourself for greater things.

BRIEF STORY

Creating a Learning Program

I gave training a lot of thought and what I noticed was that there was never enough in the budget, or people wouldn't take time out of their busy schedules to attain new knowledge. I asked myself how I could change this and come up with a creative way to get virtual training to approximately 2,500 people. My goal was to develop an automated training system that would enable employees to tap into teaching modules.

I started with a sketch on a scrap piece of paper. Like many other things I did in the business world, I would dream something up on a rough sketch and scribble thoughts on how I wanted to bring my ideas to life. Then I partnered with employees who knew me well and could help me solidify my vision to start making it look like something possible. Together, we would mature the product until it started to take shape. I was always amazed how a brainstorm could eventually turn into a really cool product.

As this training module began to take shape, I could see how excited my team was getting and the confidence they had this tool was going to be a game changer for business management's training objectives.

As I was dreaming up this training tool, I thought back to my early and mid-career years when I was seeking substantial training that wouldn't take weeks and months to attain. I also wanted to build the training around many subjects through connecting the dots to a full view of all of the business disciplines.

My goal was to furnish the workforce the ability to learn many things and round out their sphere of knowledge. I'm convinced that I would have accelerated my career growth if I would have had a learning tool like this to learn lots of different things.

Most people like myself didn't even know some of these skills were out there. I was determined that this process of developing the tool would generate enthusiasm and employee engagement across many employees who would be required to develope the required teaching modules. I liked to call them "subject matter experts." When we began to solicit employee participation we saw that people were really excited and wanted to be part of this initiative. My team and I then needed to find a way to keep this whole process organized, disciplined and consistent. Our next step was to design a common format, where we would have things that would include the subject matter expert's name, contact information, subject, creation date, etc.

The next item would be the presentation tutorial. Once again, we wanted to ensure that we had consistency in the format of the charts, depth of information and the quality of the final products. In the early stages, we had about twenty-five subjects. When I left the company, we had over one hundred different teaching modules.

My contacts tell me that the tool continues to grow and mature.

As we began to see that we had the beginning of strong teaching modules, we knew the next step was getting information technology involved in the maturity of the process.

The files and presentations that we created required large memory as well as the need to automate the tool so all employees could tap into the system with simple-step directions. Believe me, I'm making this sound a lot simpler than it was; frankly, it started to get fairly complicated! With the help of our information technology group our tool was really taking shape. In addition to the valuable content, I wanted to make sure that the tool was intuitive and user-friendly. Our team felt a sense of great accomplishment, but I told them that we needed to go to the next step: one-hour video presentations so that employees using the system could read ahead and then watch the subject matter experts. Their supporting panels could then teach their subject. I still wasn't completely happy and included a cross section of business employees into the video taping of the teaching modules and had them ask pre-determined questions to the experts. As I mentioned, this wasn't just a teaching moment; it was a great employee engagement moment.

Once we went live with the system online, we conducted feedback surveys. We received great reviews and great suggestions that we often incorporated. My dream that was on that scratch piece of paper had come to light! It was one of my most rewarding experiences.

We tracked the participation rates every week and found that more than 50% of the organization was logging into the system. I then knew we had a winner.

I'm sure like most executives, we will soon become a distant memory for our employees, but my hope is that this would be part of my legacy and something that will make Northrop Grumman a better company.

Every time I presented this initiative, whether it was to working groups or senior executives, I always felt great pride and satisfaction. It was a defining moment for me to launch this tool and I hope it continues to grow and mature for many years to come.

Here, I want to underscore the value and importance of knowledge and to encourage you to explore things that you know little about. Diversification of talent will serve you well. As you grow through the organization and become part of the leadership team, you will be a stronger leader because of your broad knowledge base.

Learn as much as you can as fast as you can.

CHAPTER 10

Rise and Shine—Always Be Leading

"Leadership is about making others better as a result of your
presence and making sure that impact lasts in your absence."

—SHERYL SANDBERG

MY EXPERIENCE HAS always been that good leaders are clear
from the start and they mature and cultivate the team as they
move forward.

The biggest suggestion I can make is for all leaders to
value their team. A happy and engaged workforce will have a
much greater chance of delivering strong results. It's easy to get
entangled in the demanding expectations of every day. While
driving hard for results, keep a perspective that your team could
be losing steam and feeling overwhelmed. Good leaders need to
pause and re-energize their team at this point and reassure them
that you understand the stress that's affecting them. Taking the
time to meet with the team and take a short break from the
intensity will pay great dividends. Continuous reinforcement
and perspective will help keep the team focused and motivated.

As a leader, I would make it a priority to let the team know that I was ultimately responsible and when required to, I would roll up my sleeves and work side by side with them to solve problems or smash roadblocks. During the early stages of a project, I would set the tone and frame the objectives/timeframe and then get out of the way and let them perform.

I would also reinforce the point that they could come to me anytime. Here again, there is a fine line between letting the team run too far without a lot of input and being on top of them constantly. Balance! So that I didn't over power them and stifle their creativity, I would ask them periodically for a brief status. This would also give them an opportunity to ask for help if required. They needed to know that if there was a hard decision to be made or they needed me to push my weight around to get them help and support, I would be there for them.

Candidly, there were many times where the pressure from my superiors would get quite stressful and I needed to get them information and recommendations. Knowing that my team was working hard and sometimes hitting roadblocks, it became a delicate balancing act for me to keep my team motivated, yet keep the pressure on them. I would count on my instincts to tell me if I needed to reprioritize my day and hunker down with my team to help get them to the finish line.

Whenever I found myself in this position, I would do my best to make it a learning experience for everyone rather than just another crazy deadline. Specifically, I would usually pause and explain to them why I was going down a particular path and the reasons why I was making certain decisions. I would also ask them as a group if that made sense and if they thought it was a good way to proceed, knowing that we were about to run out of time.

Most of the time, they would thank me and say that they could get a better answer/solution if they had more time, but given they didn't, they thought we were good to proceed. I also explained that it was my job to deliver the information to the next level of management with confidence, but to also reinforce that we could refine the information going forward and give them an update if warranted. At this point, my team would understand the objective and reasoning and they would be all in.

I wanted them to also be assured that the integrity of our work was our No. 1 priority. No matter how much pressure we were under, there would be absolutely no compromise when it came to ethics.

I immensely enjoyed working side by side with my teams when required, but it also helped me gain their support and respect. Periodically throughout a project, I would send individuals or the entire team a note thanking them for their professionalism and dedication. This would go a long way. Remember, we all like praise for what we do! I would often copy their managers and directors so they would get a broader feeling of appreciation.

This would frequently generate a response from their immediate leader in the organization, giving the employee even greater satisfaction that their hard work was being recognized across the enterprise. I found this to be an effective way to connect several employees through positive recognition.

Another great learning experience I had at Wharton involved the time we spent on leadership in organizations. My class was made up of executives from around the world with diverse backgrounds, positions and industries.

The one thing that we all agreed on was the importance of leadership in any organization. Truly good leaders are difficult to find. During our sessions on this topic, we had numerous experts come in to share their expertise. These sessions generated lots of discussion and diverse thoughts and at times, a significant amount of spirited debate. I learned so much and it was incredibly impactful to the way I looked at leadership going forward. One thing we agreed upon was that highly engaged workforces are the happiest and most effective over the long run.

<u>LEADERSHIP AND THE SYMPHONY</u>

One of the most memorable sessions regarding leadership was when the conductor of the Philadelphia Symphony came to spend the day with us and give his perspective regarding leadership and teamwork.

When we heard that a conductor was coming to help us think through leadership, we were all a little perplexed. What could a symphony conductor know about leadership as it relates to the business world? I can assure you we didn't say that at the end of his time with us.

This was an eye-opening experience. I remember him furnishing each one of us with a conductor's baton. He asked us if we knew what a conductor really could accomplish with this simple tool. He gave us the answer to that question and kept us fully engaged for the entire day. He explained the importance of leadership when leading a symphony of extremely talented, strong, egotistical professionals. He made endless thought-provoking points supplemented with videos of live symphony performances.

He did this to clearly emphasize how he, as a conductor, would control the flow of the performance by his movements and eye contacts. When he did this, we could clearly see how he controlled the entire flow of the performance. There was no doubt that he was the leader of this highly technical musical ensemble.

As much as we all could value his leadership, we were still wondering how we could relate this to running a business. We had a great exchange of Q &A with this gentleman. He went on to describe the complexity of the group/organization of musicians that he was responsible for leading.

There were numerous instruments involved with different levels of experience and expertise. He also got us to understand that each group thought they were the most important to the success of the symphony. It was his job to convince them that they were all extremely talented and valued but without them working as a team, they would never succeed.

The conductor had to deal with many strong personalities within a large, highly talented group of people.

His No. 1 priority was to gain their respect and entice them to value the role and the expertise that everyone contributed and that he had to successfully integrate to result in one free-flowing, beautiful performance. He was extremely forthcoming and made it crystal clear to us that there was plenty of confrontational moments where he was required during practice to diffuse and bring the group back into unison. The trick he said was to practice and debate behind the scenes, always striving for perfection.

The conductor's mission was to lead the group through the challenges and then take a stand on the best way forward, convincing the overall team that this was the best path for success.

I really related to this as did most leaders because we are frequently put into roles that involve directing technical experts in their field. The conductor shared with us how important it was that each performer value their coworkers and know that the conductor took responsibility to ensure that they always stayed in sync. Throughout my years in large leadership roles, I never forget the lessons I learned that day and how leadership comes in many shapes, sizes and forms, and each situation is somewhat unique.

To drive home all of the incredible learning lessons from this highly skilled leader, we attended one of his Philadelphia orchestra performances. Not only was it a great cultural event but one of learning. I assessed every move the conductor made that night, and it was magical to see how he directed the performance and the way in which each musician reacted to his powerful, but subtle hand and body movements.

Throughout the performance, I could clearly see how much respect the orchestra members had for the conductor. I intently focused on some of the musicians to see how they were making eye contact with the conductor. You could see how much esteem they all had for the conductor. This wasn't just some guy moving his body and baton around. He was an established musician himself, who had a unique ability/talent to take a group of individually highly talented musicians and integrate them together to create a magical performance.

I know from experience how hard it is leading a group of talented counterparts. In my role as a CFO, I was often required to take the lead of many of my colleagues. These individuals were quite talented and had significant responsibilities and leadership skills of their own. Because of my position, I was often required to lead and set the tone for many of our corporate executive reviews with the company CEO and CFO. Each of these business unit's vice presidents would have a speaking role in the reviews.

A fair amount of their presentations centered around strategy, risk management, financial performance, etc. It was my job to support and advise the VP and general manager of the division in orchestrating the integration of the presentations so they looked seamless and were totally connected.

I had the view of the entire business across the division enabling me to ensure there was strong linkage across the division. I also had a clear understanding of what the company CFO would be looking for and his expectations and concerns.

During our practice reviews there would be a fair amount of debate and sometimes aggressive behavior. Like the conductor, I had to deal with strong personalities. As I learned from the conductor, you must recognize how valuable your colleagues are to the success of the business as a whole and that they have enormous pride in their work and capabilities. I always had the conductor's advice in the back of my head, especially during instances when there were tense moments with one or multiple colleagues. It helped give me perspective and taught me that I needed to be a good listener. That advice surely helped me during these tough situations. He stressed that you need to remain calm and open minded, as difficult as that may be at the moment.

Like the orchestra, our leadership team exhausted our differences during our practice sessions. I ultimately needed to make the final decisions and recommendations to the general manager on which way I thought we needed to proceed.

I was excellent at messaging and making sure that we did not contradict one another, which is a sure recipe to get the corporate executives nervous, creating uncertainty and loss of confidence in our team. During our final dry run, I would let the team know that I would set the stage for them and work hard at making sure to prepare the corporate executive team for the presentations that would follow me without stealing their thunder. I had the confidence of the CEO and CFO, which helped us as we transitioned to the VP of each business within the division.

During the vice presidents' individual presentations, like the conductor, when required, I would jump back into the discussion to keep us on course and clear up any misunderstandings. I know my counterparts did not want help in their speaking part to the CEO, so I was sensitive of that and made sure I interceded only when necessary and with quick, precise comments.

This was a skill that I learned to perfect and like the conductor, I pulled it off most often with little to no fanfare. My teammates, although sometimes reluctant, thanked me for adding clarity and helping secure an excellent team performance. It should also be noted that at times, I only needed to make eye contact with one of my coworkers and they knew that they needed to pause what they were saying, and in some instances, look to me to jump in. We knew each other well and even though we all had relatively large egos, we respected each other's talents and realized that the team was bigger than any one individual.

Often, the CEO/CFO and other executive members would compliment us for our thoroughness and professionalism. Thankfully, like the orchestra, they didn't have a view of us in practice, because it was sometimes an ugly scene!

Key advice from the conductor:

◆ Earn the respect and confidence of your team.

◆ Always be fair and respectful regardless of position in the organization.

◆ Clearly present your vision for the team.

◆ Get to know each team member; understand what makes them tick.

◆ Understand the strengths and weaknesses of each team member.

◆ Always give praise and recognition when earned.

◆ Don't criticize individuals in a large group setting.

◆ Listen to the team's suggestions as a group and individually; then make the final decision and explain your reasoning.

◆ Never lose control; be firm but compassionate.

◆ Practice for perfection.

◆ Make it clear from the start that a team can only succeed if everyone is on the same page.

◆ If you are not willing to be flexible for the team you will no longer be on the team; leave your ego at home.

◆ Do all your coaching during practice. On performance day, play the game with a clear head and stay focused.

As it related to the conductor in his leadership role, he told his team to look for his leadership during their performance and if for some reason something was wrong, stay focused on him and his direction. His job was to successfully keep professional musicians focused at all times. When the team took his lead, they could recover from a mistake without the audience ever knowing it took place.

From that day forward, I kept the conductor's baton on my desk as a visual reminder of what I learned from that spectacular experience. Needless to say, this was another great learning experience that I was fortunate to have at my time at Wharton.

Now that I have described this conductor's leadership role, I will give you an example of how I utilized this knowledge in my division CFO leadership position and how it relates to experiences I had in leadership roles at Northrop Grumman.

As a CFO, each quarter, I was responsible for briefing the corporate CEO/COO/CFO regarding my division's quarter-end forecast and future year projections, as well as addressing significant risks and opportunities. This was usually a stressful time as financial data would come in at various times of the day just preceding my date to brief the corporate leadership team. These briefings required a high level of fidelity and clear messaging.

Getting the financial data and future forecasts warranted lots of reviews with my project business directors, division controller and financial manager.

If I could paint a visual for you at crunch time, it would look somewhat chaotic and unorganized. To a casual observer they would never think that we would successfully come out with a product that would be of the caliber expected to brief the corporate executive team.

My job was similar to the symphony conductor in that we would assemble in my office with my core division financial leadership team. I had a white board and a large TV screen to review our slides real-time.

The white board was full of notes and actions as we worked our way through the process, which involved the construction of approximately twenty-five slides full of numbers graphs, pictures, etc. My allotted time to deliver my messages was usually around thirty or forty minutes. Content was obviously critical, with messaging, a close number two. We would likely spend two full days constructing our final charts and then I was on an airplane from New York or Florida to Los Angeles for the review.

Now, picture four or five of us in my office trying to build our story with final data coming in on the fly all day long. By the nature of the business, most of the data is real-time. I would have my executive assistant, whose work station was right outside my office doing her daily activities for me and also running in and out of my office with copies of inputs and collecting data slides from each business unit.

She would also begin to integrate slides where possible. At the same time, we would have different business directors on the phone as we would be spraying them with questions and clarification pertaining to their real-time inputs. My financial manager would also be in the conference room next to me reviewing data with accounting and his financial teams that resided on each major program.

To complicate things even further, we had an East Coast-West Coast time difference to deal with. We would also be conducting net meetings with my directors so they could review the modifications to their original inputs. My executive assistant would also be shuffling people in and out of my office bringing us data and answers to questions.

On top of this, I was still required to leave this activity during certain times to attend meetings and take phone calls from my bosses. As you can imagine, there was always lots of moving pieces and a deadline staring at us. My job as the "conductor" was to set the goals, time line, assignments, etc. I would be dealing with experts from across the division and had to keep them focused on my mission as they would be distracted by other leaders on their programs.

Numerous times, I had to perform conflict management. Everyone had the best of intentions, but when a team is tired and stressed negative situations can start to materialize.

As I mentioned, it wouldn't look organized to an outsider, but my division team was always watching and hearing my direction without a word sometimes ever even spoken.

This doesn't mean that there weren't points of confrontation between us because there surely were those moments. We would work long hours knowing that this presentation was going to receive tough scrutiny and it had to be well thought out and executed. I balanced being extremely aggressive at times and then rapidly reverting back to being calm and rational. In a strange way, I guess I loved the challenge and the goal of impressing our executives with our performance and messaging.

Like the conductor, I just needed to give a quick signal or brief direction to my team as we were well-versed on what needed to be accomplished in a short timeframe. To make it more complicated, I needed to keep the division general manager informed to the way the numbers we were developing and how I was going to construct good messaging and potentially bad news.

Whenever someone entered my office, they would just shake their head, wondering how I was going to pull this off. Someone once described it as an organized well-oiled machine always in full motion. Now that I look back, it really was a sight to be seen.

Whenever practical, I would have one or two of my mentees participate so that they could see the proverbial "sausage" being made and then bring them along to shadow me when I presented. To a person, they would tell me it was like a movie being produced with lots of stuff landing on the production floor.

I never forgot the advice from the conductor: practice, fix, practice, fix, then the performance will go great.

As in the case of the conductor, everything that happened during practice we would flush out problems and concerns, ensuring that we had answers for every imaginable question that could come at me during the executive review. This is where preparation and perfection pay off.

I can't reinforce the point enough how important it is that you have a great team who embrace and respect your leadership.

BRIEF STORY

Leaderhip in Crisis

I feel compelled to share a recent story regarding teamwork and leadership that I witnessed during my dad's recovery in the hospital from a serious open-heart surgery experience. From the minute my dad was wheeled into the Intensive Care Unit of one the most prestigious university teaching hospitals in the world, I was blown away by the care and integrated performance and the skill of the unit's team.

My dad is eighty-six years old and had two valves repaired and a bypass performed, requiring very close and expert medical care. It exemplified the true meaning of a well-oiled machine involving highly talented people. As I spent the next eight days with my dad, I couldn't help but think about how I was going to add this experience to my book, as it was such a compelling example of teamwork and leadership!

My dad was the client and he required the best to get him back to his old self. They did a magnificent job and he and our family were extremely pleased with the entire team.

This team was of the highest caliber. They truly cared about the welfare of their patients and you could quickly get the sense that they loved their jobs, though at times, they were under extreme stress.

My biggest takeaway was their unwavering commitment to excellence and the value they placed on teamwork. Remember, these are highly educated and skilled people required to keep their individual egos at home. I could see that it was about the patient and the only way for their unit to be of world-class stature was for them to perform as an integrated team.

Whether it was the unit'ss director (lead physician), resident doctors, physician assistants, registered nurses, physical therapist, facilities, housekeeping, etc. they all had a role in keeping this unit humming in unison.

The experience brought me back to my days at Wharton when the symphony orchestra conductor told us how he was able to lead a group of highly talented people. No matter what level of stature they had in this unit they had mutual respect for each other. I remember one day when we requested a new bed for my dad that would help him with his back.

They ordered the bed and when it was delivered the facilities supervisor made sure everything was done with minimal disturbance to my dad and the family. The nurse worked closely with him to get everything rearranged and this was not easy due to the complexity of the equipment needed for an open-heart patient recovery.

They both worked fluidly and you could hear and see how they respected each other and how this wasn't the first time they had to work together as a team. It may seem like a small thing, but in this critical care environment, it was a big thing and we all took notice.

As you can imagine, intensive care units contain lots of moving parts with many high-tech pieces of equipment being transferred around the unit. There were certain times during our eight days in ICU that we found ourselves in my dads' room and an announcement would come over the system locking down the unit to deal with an emergency-code patient. This can be a scary event to see going down. Within seconds, certain doctors and nurses went into full emergency mode. It was unbelievable to see how the director of the unit assembled the specific skills required to support him. Hardly a word was spoken and the necessary equipment was being hooked up and numerous medications were being administered.

For a medical lay person, I was overwhelmed by their calmness and professionalism with only a moment's notice.

This may be an "extreme" example of team work, leadership, communications and focus. Still, I needed to share it because it underscores just how valuable it is to the success of any business to be prepared and embrace the value of teamwork to strengthen the overall performance of the business.

I should also mention that the staff that was not engaged with the emergency patient were also working seamlessly to cover for their teammates, ensuring that the unit continue to operate at the highest level of efficiency. It was amazingly seamless. I couldn't help from taking notice of this phenomenon.

As a corporate business leader, it impressed me so much and I broke it down in my mind as to how this all just happened without any major glitches. I would sum it up by saying it was all about leadership, the culture that was established, and the dedication and practice required to ensure that they performed at the highest level. Once the emergency concluded, the unit went back to normal operation like nothing ever happened.

This experience will stay with me forever. I really wanted to frame it for you so you could think about how you would build your team as a leader or what type of team you would want to work with in your career.

Another example that I experienced in this ICU also centered around teamwork and mutual respect for team-mates' opinions and recommendations. Every morning, the staff supporting my dad's recovery would gather just outside his room and review his stats, recovery status and plan going forward.

While going through this review, they invited us to listen to the dialogue and encouraged us to ask any and all ques-tions. This was full transparency at its best. For the purpose of painting this picture for you, the participants of this daily review centered around the unit director, anesthesiologist, two residents, physician assistant and the attending registered nurse.

As this was a teaching university hospital it valued the open discussion and sometimes change of direction, but it was always executed in a manner of teaching and learning, display of how to do things better and to make sure the best treatment was being utilized.

Remember, failure was not an option. The process was for the attending resident to brief the director with the status of the patient and any changes in vitals or medications.

They would also lay out the plan for the next day(s) ahead. Lots of information was being shared and the staff would weigh in, always being respectful to the opinions of their teammates.

The director would let the conversation flow, interjecting where required to help the team pause and giving them input that may make them think about going in another direction.

I was always impressed with the knowledge and focus the attending nurse was with my dad's condition and his well-being. At first, I thought the doctors would just pass over the nurse's input, but to my pleasant surprise, they did just the opposite. It became quite apparent during these reviews how much respect the doctors had for the nurse as she interjected her thoughts and expertise. They realized that their strength came from their combined knowledge and experience.

Even though there were five doctors involved, they depended on the attending nurse, who knew my father best. She was working the details on an hourly basis whereas the doctors observed from a thousand feet. This was not a typical post-operation nursing person; she was someone highly trained in cardio intensive care.

I watched them administer approximately fifteen medications and endless tubes and wires. I never saw anything like it. One mistake could create a possible life or death condition.

The doctors valued the nurses for their education, dedication and skill. When that happens, the organization and the customer are the big winners.

One day, I was chatting with the director of the unit and I complimented her and told her how impressed I was with the knowledge and the compassion of her staff and most of all, the nursing and support staff.

I was blown away when she made it clear to how important her nursing staff was to the success of the team and how valuable their input is in giving the patient the best chance for a full recovery.

I should also mention that the surgeon who visited daily also highly complimented the unit's performance and that my dad couldn't be in better hands.

How great it would be if corporate leaders could observe how this system works and the true critical benefits of leadership and teamwork. Most of all, it would help corporate leaders realize how important all levels of the team are and that they should value them accordingly, as they are the heartbeat (no pun intended) to the success of the business.

Like many other skills, leadership is a work in process. You need to start out small and take the lead on a small project. There are a few important steps to take towards becoming an effective leader:

◆ Strive to stretch your capabilities and think outside the box.

◆ Create and cultivate a team, ultimately which you will lead.

◆ Think through your strategy with your team.

◆ Create a plan of action. Document your plan and then reduce to specific tasks.

◆ Track the plan with a schedule and metrics. This doesn't have to be fancy.

◆ Be open to all ideas.

◆ Encourage creativity, but be realistic.

◆ Manage the clock; time can pass by rapidly without much being accomplished. It requires strong time management skills. Avoid getting stuck which leads to panic.

◆ Dry-run your preliminary plan with your boss to solicit input and feedback.

◆ Remember good planning leads to good execution.

◆ Don't be afraid to make changes throughout the process.

◆ Documentation is vital.

◆ Details and process matter.

◆ Trust your team.

◆ Be a good listener.

Once you rise to a leadership role, you will quickly learn that your team is your lifeline. Whether you are leading or managing three or 300 people, your team will make or break you. Foster an environment of openness and exchange of information. In terms of team building, these approaches are of utmost importance:

- Meet with them regularly.
- Solicit their recommendations.
- Emphasize "people first" philosophy.
- Share your vision and operating philosophy.
- Care about your employees and show an interest in them.
- Be honest with your team.
- Support your team.
- Provide training opportunities.
- Advocate for them when deserving to move up the corporate ladder.
- Make them comfortable, letting them know that they can come to you.
- Reinforce the importance of integrity.
- Encourage employees to have a coach and a mentor.
- Require hard work and dedication while also encouraging and setting an example for work-life balance.
- A happy and engaged workforce will have a much better chance of delivering strong results.
- Make the hard decisions.
- Never throw your team under the bus; you are part of your team.
- Lead the team and then get out of the way; let them perform.
- When you get praise from superiors, pass the recognition down.
- Periodically send your team gratitude notes for a job well done. Copy your superiors so they get to recognize performance, too.

CHAPTER 11

Powerful Moments, Endless Possibilities

"If someone offers you an amazing opportunity and you're not sure
you can do it, say yes-then learn how to do it later."

—RICHARD BRANSON

SECURING YOUR FIRST professional position is only the beginning of a life-long career journey full of great and exciting
opportunities. Learn something new every day and differentiate yourself from the competition by continuously growing
through hard work, dedication, education and on-the-job,
real-time experiences. Making mistakes and taking some risk is
not a bad thing. Don't allow yourself to get overly comfortable
and complacent. It may feel good at the time, but I can assure you
that time will pass by rapidly and you will wake up one day and
wonder how others gained success and stature and you didn't
seem to move anywhere. Investing in yourself is essential. Like
most things in life, success requires sacrifice and commitment.

As I reflect back and retrace my steps, I can clearly see where
I made good decisions that paid significant personal dividends.

When being totally honest with myself, I can also see where I made missteps that could have easily been avoided if I paid more attention.

Like most leaders and executives, I was committed to taking charge of my career and charting a course of action. Throughout the years, I was determined to succeed, as well as being cognizant of the people supporting me. I always felt that if my team was successful, I would be successful.

This served me well throughout my career and my teams always gave me 110%. I found that the more I cared about the wellbeing of my team and the enterprise, the more I thrived. Senior leaders will recognize your talents and commitment and most often, you will be rewarded. Don't get overly fixated on your level in the organization. Instead, focus on the performance of the business and your contributions to its wellbeing. Even at the most junior level, leadership will recognize that you are different than most and that you embody a strong work ethic, integrity, commitment and personality, enabling you to grow through the ranks of the organization.

Try to pause once a week and evaluate if you learned something new, had a noteworthy experience or contributed to something that will make you a little more prepared for the next step in your career. A technique I used was to document accomplishments. Some may have been small things and others were significant game changers. As I mentioned in the resume preparation section, when I felt there was a skill or achievement that better described me, I would add it to my resume and remove something less impressive. This would keep me motivated—I was the type that needed to see progress! I'm a firm believer in writing things down so you can visualize and determine if it's important and valuable to add to your personnel marketing tool.

It basically comes down to having a plan and monitoring it on a regular basis. Make a game out of it. Keep it simple and have some fun with it. This is not rocket science, but most people never take the time to do the tasks described in the 6 P's.

Don't allow yourself to get bogged down in your everyday routine, stretch yourself, take chances and don't put things off. Time will go by quickly, so capitalize on every day.

Keep your eyes on the rapidly moving target. Have fun and always find ways to improve yourself. Most of all, help others throughout your career. You will find this to be enormously rewarding. I can truly say that the most rewarding memories I have are knowing that I helped shape many of our future leaders. Now get on with it, and accomplish great things.

ABOUT THE AUTHOR

RICHARD LEO was Vice President and CFO for Military Aircraft Systems (MAS), a multi-billion-dollar division at Northrop Grumman Aerospace Systems, a premier provider of manned and unmanned aircraft, space systems and advanced technologies critical to our nation's security. His functional responsibilities included 600+ personnel, contracts, pricing and estimating, cost/schedule management, financial planning/reporting, resource management, overhead rates management, long range strategic planning, new business capture and business management.

Before retiring November 2017, Leo had 37 years of experience in the aerospace industry.

Leo graduated from Dowling College in 1980 with a bachelor's degree in business administration and business management and a minor in banking, real estate and insurance. He earned a master's (MBA) in business management from Dowling College in 1994. He also completed the University of Pennsylvania Wharton School of Business Advanced Management Program in 2006.

A frequent lecturer at colleges and universities nationwide, Leo helps students transition from college to corporate America.

ACKNOWLEDGEMENTS

MY PROFESSIONAL CAREER was a long journey involving many twists and turns. Throughout the years, I always had the unwavering support of my wonderful family. My job required long hours, significant travel and lots of time away from home. I was always able to do this knowing that everything at home was in the best of hands. My loving wife of thirty-one years, Carmel-Lina, has been the bedrock of support for me throughout these many years. She has always kept our family and home running smoothly without missing a beat, while having to pick up the slack as I traveled and worked many long hours and quite often, weekends. She also did an incredible job raising our two children, Rich and Jacqueline, who I couldn't be prouder of. In my view, real success is knowing that you have raised caring, intelligent, respectful children who make you glow with pride. I'm also very proud of their early professional career success and I'm extremely confident that they will both have bright, rewarding futures and ultimately, turn out to be great leaders.

I also want to recognize my daughter-in-law, Jordan, who I'm also proud of. She is on her way to a bright, professional future and most of all, I'm glad that she is part of our family.

Making this all happen required enormous sacrifice from CarmelLina, and I can't thank her enough for the great family she has nurtured. Her unwavering dedication, sacrifice, commitment, love and patience were beyond anyone's expectations. I'm an extremely lucky and blessed guy!

I also want to thank my parents, Richard and Frieda, and my mother-in-law, Lilly, for their great support throughout the many years. Knowing that they were there to help our family always gave me great comfort. I can't thank them enough for their love and support. There is nothing more important than family!

In my professional world, I was extremely fortunate to have had numerous mentors who gave me great advice, guidance and encouragement. I was lucky to have wonderful bosses who advocated for me, as well as great administrative assistants. In addition, the team members that worked with me during every stage of my career always made me look good. Way too many people to specifically call out, but they know who they are. My thanks to all of you!

Writing this book and getting it published was more daunting than I had ever anticipated. I want to thank my daughter and my wife for the endless hours they supported me while listening to me read endless segments of the manuscript at every stage of its maturity. Without their patience, support, advice and encouragement, this book would have never happened. I also want to thank my son and daughter for their input in creating the title and subtitle of the book. Once again, my thanks to my family for supporting me and enabling me to create this book.

I also want to thank Candi Cross, my collaborator and professional writer. Her upbeat personality and her incredible writing skills turned my manuscript from a dream to reality. She is a true professional and a wonderful teammate. With Candi's recommendation, I was fortunate to also partner with Glen Edelstein, a professional book designer. He did an incredible job of making the cover pop with excitement. There is nothing better than having great professionals on your team!

Finally, I want to thank my wife and children for believing in me, which means the world to me, and I can't thank them enough.